MAKE OVER YOUR SEX LIFE... TONIGHT!

*Hot, Fast, Erotic Fixes . . .
and Sensuous Stories to
Get Things Started*

MAKE OVER YOUR SEX LIFE... TONIGHT!

Hot, Fast, Erotic Fixes . . .
and Sensuous Stories to
Get Things Started

SUSAN CRAIN BAKOS

NEW AMERICAN LIBRARY

New American Library
Published by New American Library, a division of
Penguin Group (USA) Inc., 375 Hudson Street, New York, New York 10014, USA
Penguin Group (Canada), 90 Eglinton Avenue East, Suite 700, Toronto,
Ontario M4P 2Y3, Canada (a division of Pearson Penguin Canada Inc.)
Penguin Books Ltd., 80 Strand, London WC2R 0RL, England
Penguin Ireland, 25 St. Stephen's Green, Dublin 2,
Ireland (a division of Penguin Books Ltd.)
Penguin Group (Australia), 250 Camberwell Road, Camberwell, Victoria 3124,
Australia (a division of Pearson Australia Group Pty. Ltd.)
Penguin Books India Pvt. Ltd., 11 Community Centre, Panchsheel Park,
New Delhi - 110 017, India
Penguin Group (NZ), cnr Airborne and Rosedale Roads, Albany,
Auckland 1310, New Zealand (a division of Pearson New Zealand Ltd.)
Penguin Books (South Africa) (Pty.) Ltd., 24 Sturdee Avenue,
Rosebank, Johannesburg 2196, South Africa

Penguin Books Ltd., Registered Offices: 80 Strand, London WC2R 0RL, England

First published by New American Library, a division of Penguin Group (USA) Inc.

First Printing, October 2005
10 9 8 7 6 5 4 3 2 1

NEW AMERICAN LIBRARY and logo are trademarks of Penguin Group (USA) Inc.

LIBRARY OF CONGRESS CATALOGING-IN-PUBLICATION DATA:
    Bakos, Susan Crain.
    Make over your sex life—tonight!: hot, fast, erotic fixes—and sensuous stories to get
things started/Susan Crain Bakos.
        p. cm.
    ISBN 0-451-21407-2
1. Sex instruction.   2. Sex.   3. Sexual excitement.   I. Title.
    HQ31.B2349   2005
    613.9'6—dc22   2005010861

Set in Filosofia
Designed by Helene Berinsky

Printed in the United States of America

This book is for Tamm,
with love and gratitude
for the concept.

ACKNOWLEDGMENTS

Many thanks to my editor, Tracy Bernstein, and my agent, Janet Rosen—for their extraordinary patience and faith in this project.

Thanks to Tiffany Yates for her excellent copyediting. I am also grateful to the editors of *Redbook* magazine, who have nurtured and encouraged my sex research. A "Sex Life Makeovers" article first appeared in *Redbook*. The editors were also first to recognize that the sex technique I invented, the Orgasm Loop, was a fresh, new idea and asked me to write about it. My best magazine pieces have appeared in *Redbook* because the editors there know what they're doing when it comes to assigning and shaping sex advice articles.

Some professional associates have encouraged me in this book and many other endeavors. They include especially

Dr. Joel Block and Dr. Bob Berkowitz, and also Dr. Patti Britton. I learned a great deal about the uses of fantasy in Sex Life Makeovers from Dr. Carole Pasahow, whose own work in that area is brilliant and groundbreaking.

My closest friends have been more important to me in this past year than ever before. I thank them for their friendship, their emotional support, their faith in me—and for being so much fun. They are Joe Rinaldi, Alex Zola, Carolyn Males, and Michael and Barbara Hasamear.

To the Sex Life Makeover participants—thank you over and over again. What great sports you all are!

A special thank-you to my sister, Ellen, who is always there for me, my niece, Shawn, my daughter-in-law, Tamm, and the three little ones who bring so much joy to our lives: Iva Marie, Richard Charles, and Marcella Catherine.

And kisses to my lovers, past and present. I don't think I could write about sex if I hadn't been lucky enough to have had wonderful lovers.

CONTENTS

Does Your Sex Life
Need a Makeover?

Makeovers! They are every woman's (and man's) version of the fairy godmother's wand. We all want a piece of the magic.

You could transform your life today in many ways: by cutting off your long brown hair, coloring it blond, and trading those basic midheel black pumps for a pair of hot pink stilettos; by turning your cluttered office into a true workspace where creativity can flourish; by painting the living room a soft, glowing orange and adding exotic pillows, art baskets, and a huge palm tree or two.

Makeovers are so appealing because they promise to change us within as well as without. We will *become* the Chic Blonde, the Writer, the Worldly Sophisticate that our new exteriors boast that we are. And, unless we fall back into our old mousy, cluttered, and drab ways again, we do transform ourselves, at least to some degree.

But can you make over your sex life that easily?

There are a lot of misconceptions about sex. One of the most popular among women is that good sex takes place only within the confines of a committed, monogamous relationship. And even achieving good sex within those narrow confines takes time and "work." When you hear the word *relationship*, the phrase *working on* won't be far behind. With luck and a weekly visit to couples therapy, you can change and improve your sex life in three to six months, provided you're both willing to "communicate" everything. You're probably not going to be that lucky, especially if your insurance doesn't cover extensive therapy. (Therapy seems to expand the outer limits of your insurance!)

Men, on the other hand, have been programmed to believe a sexual makeover is breast-enhancement surgery for the current partner—or trading that old partner for a new, younger model.

In this book I show you how to rejuvenate that tired old sex life beginning tonight, no therapy, no surgery required.

Yes, I Said: Tonight

Like popular cosmetic makeovers, Sex Life Makeovers create significant change in a short period of time. I know that the standard advice assumes you can't improve the sex without an investment of time and effort. But it's wrong!

You can, for example, learn how to have an orgasm during lovemaking faster than you can shop for a new, more flattering look. Unless you or your partner has serious psychological issues affecting sexual desire or performance or you are trying to have good sex with someone who has *never* attracted you, there's nothing wrong with your sex life that a quick and easy makeover can't fix.

As a sex journalist, sexologist, and author of five previous sex advice books, I have interviewed thousands of men and women about their intimate lives. And I hear the same complaints over and over again. So many people with the same basic problems that are really not difficult to fix! Yet what kind of advice is out there for them? Guides by therapists to creating more intimate, passionate marriages—and increasingly complicated technique guides by sexperts in competition with one another to see who can make a basic blow job the most complex erotic performance act. (When a popular sex adviser offered fifty-seven versions of the hand job, I knew sex technique advice had jumped the shark.)

That's what led me to develop the Sex Life Makeover program based on my radical idea that sex is not brain surgery.

And sex should definitely not be "work."

I've guided men and women, committed couples and dating singles, through hundreds of erotic transformations. It worked for most of them. Trust me. You can have a more sizzling sex life in less time than it takes a brunette to go blond.

How the Makeover Works

Each makeover begins with a quick fix that is so easy and produces such immediate benefits that you and your partner will be motivated by the results to follow through on the rest of the week's plan. You'll experience increased satisfaction on night one—and a real turnaround within the week. The moves are simple. Sometimes they may not work for you without a little modification. Don't worry about that. Modify a move, and if you still don't like it, go on to the next one. Feel free to borrow techniques from other makeovers.

Each chapter will present a typical sex problem/situation, give the standard solution that seldom works, and finally offer in step-by-step detail the uncommon solution. That opens into an erotic story illustrating the theme. On the assumption that you are probably tired of reading anecdotes that are really composites of the patients in therapists' practices and the people sex journalists have interviewed, I am leaving out the "Anne and John say that their sex life problem is . . ." commentary. Anne and John and their dreary life stories have been replaced by brief quote capsules here and there where tester comments are genuinely helpful—but mostly by soft-core porn that will turn you on.

The Sex Life Makeover program is based on:

- Sexy advice *and* sexy stories to stimulate desire and arousal.

- Simple directions you don't need to be a contortionist to use.
- Fresh ideas. Everything that can be said about "intimacy" has been said. And I'm going to assume you already know about sexy lingerie, flowers, and candles.
- And your commitment to do the Instant First-night Makeover as described and have sex at least twice in the following six days, using the Sex Life Makeover plan.

Relax. This is going to be fun—and not only that, it really works.

Part I ....

THE

BASIC

MAKEOVER

* *one*

"The Sex Works, but the Thrill Is Gone."

The most common complaint in relationship sex: no sizzle, excitement, mystery, suspense. The devoted couple who have shared many hours of carnal pleasure know where each other's erotic buttons are located. And they know the pattern to pressing those buttons as surely as if they were entering their PIN codes into an ATM machine for cash. Sometimes that's all we want from sex, but sometimes it's not.

Each is bored by the other's signature sex moves. Here comes her little flick of the tongue. There's his eyes-open deep kiss again. Yes, the standard moves are a predictable path to release—but she complains that he single-mindedly pursues his release down that path like Pavlov's lead dog. She wants release too—maybe even as quickly and efficiently as he does—but she also wants to feel desired and desiring.

He just wants to feel really excited again.

....

Couples therapy—on the theory that you must increase intimacy by thrashing out all your issues as they even tangentially relate to sex. ("Real nakedness is peeling back those layers of the self!" a zealous therapist told me. "Sex technique is not important! It's all about getting truly naked together!" Uh-huh. I wouldn't want to go to bed with him.)

And from the sex technique advisers: Launch a sexual self-improvement course, including goals for multiple, extended, and whole-body orgasms—on the theory that good sex takes a long, long time. ("The average woman needs twenty minutes of sustained and varied-stroke cunnilingus to reach orgasm," one author says. The average woman's partner had better find a comfortable position.)

The standard sex advice for every sex problem/issue/complaint is nearly always aimed at deepening the intimate relationship or learning complex sexual tricks. I don't want to discourage you from pursuing either course, but you don't *need* to do any of that to make over your sex life tonight, the goal in this book. Someday when you have the time you will read Proust, take a French cooking class, and learn how to make love for hours, though probably not on the same vacation.

Tonight you just want to rock-'n'-roll in bed.

The Instant First-night Makeover:
Add a Few New Twists to the
Standard Routine

1. Switch your usual steps.

For example, if you typically move from manual to oral stimulation and then to intercourse, mix it up. That alone will make the sex more interesting. And who says you can't start with intercourse as long as she is lubricated? Or that you can't stop intercourse before either reaches orgasm and play manually or orally instead?

Even changing the angle from which you perform oral sex makes a difference. If he puts his head between her open legs, he should try coming in from the side instead. To fellate him, she can straddle him backward for a change.

Couples who have been together a while perform their sexual routine as if a choreographer were exhorting them not to deviate from the pattern. Get over that! This is sex, not a chorus line.

2. Or change one external basic aspect of how you "do it."

Turn the lights off if they're normally on—and vice versa. Do it in the living room, the shower, the guest bed—anyplace but your bed. Add satin sheets. Keep your clothes on. Change something.

3. Or add a surprise adaptation to your signature sex move.

❇ Technique Tips

THE KISS

Pull back from that deep French kiss, signaling your intentions. Use the tip of your tongue in circles just inside his/her lips. Tease those lips again and again with the circling tip of your tongue. Suck them gently one at a time. And, gentlemen, repeat the move on her clitoral lips.

Use your tongue to flirt with his/her mouth. Insert tip of your tongue, pull quickly back out. In and out, in and out. Finally let your tongue play inside for a while. Pull back again.

Kiss her breasts before you kiss her lips.

FELLATIO

Instead of doing the flick around the head of his penis, flick your tongue rapidly back and forth sideways along the ridge that separates the head of the penis from the shaft.

Do "the Hoover," that sucking maneuver you use on the head of his penis, on his testicles instead, one at a time.

CUNNILINGUS

Have her leave on a pair of wispy silk panties and lick through and around them. Use the end of your chin to perform some of those tongue movements.

THE INTERCOURSE MOVE

If the female-superior (woman on top) position is your move, vary it by "riding the bull," with one hand in the air, one hand against your clitoris, and an exaggerated riding style—or by leaning forward and rubbing your breasts against his chest, nipple to nipple.

If the missionary (man on top) position is your signature move, vary it by bringing her knees to her chest and lifting up her buttocks with your hands. You will enter her at a thirty-degree angle—changing the way intercourse feels for both of you.

Nothing I've suggested in the instant makeover steps above is difficult. Yet each one of these small variations—and the many more that will occur to you or that you will find in other sections of this book—makes the sex feel new, different, exciting again. Less than 10 percent of the couples who followed my Sex Life Makeover plans came back and said, "Hey, the instant makeover didn't do anything for us."

I will almost guarantee success if you *each* make at least one change in the way you typically make love tonight.

What Sex Life Makeover Participants Say

"He unbuttoned my shirt and kissed my breasts. As he helped me out of my clothes, he kissed his way down my body. All this before ever kissing my mouth. It was electric."

"We usually get undressed together in the bedroom and chat about the kids or schedules or the bills until we're naked. Tonight I grabbed her and began groping her through her clothes. We fell on the bed and tore the clothes off one another. But she left her bra and high heels on. Wow."

"When she didn't give me that little swirl at the end of every lick around the head of my penis, I wondered what she was going to do instead. She had my attention. When she massaged my perineum and sucked my balls, I thought my head would explode."

The Sex Life Makeover Plan

These general directions apply to all the Sex Life Makeover Plans.

- The program works best if you do *something* erotic together every day or night for seven days. Maybe you don't have the time or energy to make love on day two, for example, but you can give each other a brief massage or foot rub. Hold each other and kiss tenderly, deeply, while gazing into each other's eyes before falling asleep. If you have the time to read your personal e-mail tonight, you have a few minutes for erotic or sensual contact with your sex partner.
- Do have "sex" (intercourse or manual/oral activity ending in orgasm) at least twice and preferably three or more times this week.

Here is your Sex Life Makeover plan to put the thrill back in sex:

1. Continue adapting your signature sex moves—and consider picking up a new one or two. Get more creative and playful as the week goes on.

✳ Technique Tips

FOREPLAY

Put your hand on his thigh when you're sitting side by side on the sofa or in dining room chairs. Give him a mini-massage using your fingertips and thumb. Then squeeze his thigh, move your hand up a little higher, and repeat the minimassage.

Say something nice to her, very softly into her ear. Then flick the inside of her ear with the tip of your tongue. Follow that by taking her earlobe gently between your teeth.

MANUAL STIMULATION

HERS: *Put a new spin on the classic hand-job position—one hand firmly at the base of the penis, the other (well lubricated) working the shaft up and down. Work that hand from the base up to the head in a circular, twisting motion, as if you were following a winding staircase up his penis. Then start at the bottom again. This staircase only goes one way: up.*

HIS: *Arouse her via manual stimulation by approaching her from behind in the "spooning" position. Put two lubricated fingers in the shape of a V around her clitoris. Press gently and rock her pelvis against those fingers.*

2. Energize your pelvic areas.

Practitioners of martial arts know how to focus energy. They can break boards, bricks, and blocks with their bare hands because they concentrate all the energy in their bodies into the leading edge of their hand. You can move enough energy into your pelvic area to feel more sexually alive—simply by believing you can do it. Practice once a day if you can.

Close your eyes. Imagine a spot inside your body beneath your navel. That spot is called the "inner chi," considered the energy center of the body. Now imagine that you are bringing all the energy in your body into this place. Focus on that energy. Feel it inside you, warm and glowing. The warmth radiates throughout your pelvic area, suffusing your genitals. Hold the energy in place for several minutes before allowing it to return to other places in your body.

Your pelvic area feels tingling and alive—energized.

Gain new flexibility in your pelvis by incorporating these erotic exercises into your daily life.

✳ **Technique Tips** ....

THE CAT

Get down on all fours. Inhale, becoming swaybacked, bringing your shoulders up and in and lifting your head. Now exhale, arching your upper back and tucking the pelvis in and under. Draw your diaphragm up and in and pull your anal muscles up and in. Bring your chin down toward your chest. Repeat nine times. Rest. Do another ten.

THE PELVIC ROCK (FOR HER)

Wearing sexy panties and bra, stand in front of a full-length mirror, your arms hanging loosely by your sides. Breathe deeply through your mouth, all the way down into your belly. Imagine you are breathing air into your pelvis and your vagina—and breathing it back out again.

Start a forward-and-backward rocking movement with your pelvis. Keep your chest and back relaxed, not rigid; the rocking should be centered in your pelvis. Thrust forward as you inhale; let your pelvis rock back on the exhale. Rock back and forth for three to four minutes, until you feel sexy.

3. Share erotica.

X-rated videos and DVDs are useful sex aides. But try something new—the old-fashioned approach to mental arousal. Read erotica out loud to one another. Skip to the juicy parts in racy novels. Or read the stories in this book. Pick the hot book of the moment—like *100 Strokes of the Brush* or *The Surrender*—and read a few pages each night. If you're creative, write a story together, a few paragraphs a night. You'll both be thinking about sex more often than you were before.

4. Move outside your comfort zones.

What seems dirty, naughty, forbidden, even a little scary to you? Do it.

Grab a quickie in a public place, like in the car in the back of a mall parking lot (just keep your clothes on) or a unisex bathroom stall. Try something you haven't tried before like anal sex (see page 244) or spanking or couples vibrator play (page 44). Bring each other to orgasm via phone sex.

His and Her Kegels

Many sex guides, my published books included, give instructions for Kegel exercises to strengthen the PC muscles. Really, they are essential for men as well as women! Kegels are the absolute bottom-line requirement for good sex. You will have stronger, more intense orgasms. Women will have better control of his penis during intercourse—and can do some amazing tricks by squeezing and releasing the PC muscle around his shaft.

If you aren't already practicing these exercises, start now.

Locate the pubococcygeus (PC) muscle, part of the pelvic floor in both sexes, by stopping and starting the flow of urine.

Then start with:

A SHORT KEGEL SQUEEZE. *Contract the muscle twenty times at approximately one squeeze per second. Exhale*

---

gently as you tighten only the muscles around your genitals (which includes the anus), not the muscles in your buttocks. Don't bear down when you release. Simply let go. Do two sets twice a day. Gradually build up to two sets of seventy-five per day.

Then add:

A LONG KEGEL SQUEEZE. Hold the muscle contraction for a count of three. Relax between contractions. Work up to holding for ten seconds, relaxing for ten seconds. Again start with two sets of twenty each and build up to seventy-five.

You will be doing three hundred repetitions a day of the combined short and long and be ready to add:

THE PUSH-OUT. After releasing the contraction, push down and out gently, as if you were having a bowel movement with your PC muscle. Repeat gently. No bearing down.

Now create Kegel sequences that combine long and short repetitions with push-outs.

After a month of daily repetitions of three hundred, you should have a well-developed PC muscle and can keep it that way by doing one hundred fifty sets several times a week.

And consider erotic weight lifting. Weights designed to exercise the PC muscles are available in sex toy shops and catalogs. The most common varieties are smooth eggs in varying sizes made of polished wood or smooth stone, and tiny barbells. Using your PCs, you pull the weights into the vagina and push them back out again. Follow the directions accompanying the weights.

✳ Revenge Sex

He was cheating on her. Maybe he wasn't seeing all or even any of these women in the flesh, but he was cheating on her just the same. How much time did he waste on this nonsense every day? Sitting alone in her office after the rest of the staff had left for the day, she felt like a private detective in a film noir.

Amanda could not believe what she was reading in Brian's saved e-mails. From a woman who signed herself "Dirty Girl": *Ram your big cock up my ass . . . I want to feel you hard inside my ass. . . . I want you to make me cry, big boy . . . make me whimper.* And from another woman: *Oh, yes, yes, shoot your come on my breasts. I'm rubbing it into my aching nipples now . . .*

A few short months ago she would never have thought to spy on Brian by accessing his private e-mails. After two of her friends had caught their husbands masturbating to cyberporn and another discovered her live-in boyfriend was seeing a woman he'd met in a sex chat room, she was obsessed with the idea of checking up on Brian. Now she had the goods on him. Her cheeks were warm and her breathing was rapid and shallow. What was she going to do with this information?

"They're all sick fucks," her friend Lanie said. "I'd leave mine, but where would I find one any healthier?"

Where indeed?

She jumped at the rapping on her glass door, looked up, and was startled to see Jay, a coworker. "Hey," she said, closing her laptop. "I thought you went home."

"Went out for a drink and came back." He cast a shrewd glance from her face to the laptop. "Problems?" he asked.

She felt her throat closing up, and before the tears came she asked huskily, "Want to go back out for another drink?"

Walking to the bar, he put his arm around her shoulders and pulled her close to his side. She could smell his scent, sandalwood and something else, maybe musk, and feel the strong muscles in his arms. They'd been attracted to each other since he came to the firm a little over a year ago.

"Tell me about it," he said as soon as they were settled into opposite sides of a dark corner booth. She kicked off her high heels, then ran the side of her foot up and down his calf on the outside of his leg. "Feels nice," he said, reaching across the table to take her hand.

"I think my husband is cheating on me," she said, running her foot up and down the inside of his leg now. She watched his eyes cloud over with desire. "I was reading his e-mails when you knocked on my door." She rested her feet in his lap, her toes curved over the bulge in his pants.

"Electronic spying," he said, his eyes laughing at her. The waitress set their glasses of wine down in front of them. He lifted his in salute to her. "Resourceful. So what are you going to do about it?"

"I don't know," she said.

With her toes, she massaged his erection. He put his hand in his lap, caressed her toes, pulled his zipper down. She wrapped her feet around his erection. His penis felt silky through her stockings.

"I want to suck you," she said.

She saw his eyes widen in surprise as she ducked down under the table. His penis, large and throbbing, bobbed in front of her, its lovely pale head glistening. She clasped it in both hands and guided it into her mouth. He put his hand on the back of her head.

She imagined some woman taking Brian's penis into her mouth the way she was taking Jay's—and the thought excited her wildly.

Swirling her tongue around the head, she felt her power. She imagined his face, struggling to remain composed, as she sucked him into her mouth, flicked her tongue across his frenulum, and tickled his perineum with her nails. He was so big and alive in her mouth, but she was in charge of him. When she felt him near ejaculation, she was thrilled. The hot semen gushed down the back of her throat.

When she came up from under the table, she was damp with sweat. Her lipstick, she knew, was smeared, and probably her mascara too. She didn't care.

"I feel like a real woman," she said, taking a gulp of wine.

"Oh, God," he whispered. His eyes had the glazed expression of a man who is happily spent. "You're a real woman, all right. That was amazing."

"We'll do it again," she promised, though she wasn't at all sure that they would.

He held her hand, stroking it, as he told her how wonderful she was and how much he wanted to fuck her. After the second glass of wine, she was ready to go home. Brian was waiting for her.

"Where have you been?" he asked, clearly annoyed. "I've left three messages on your cell. Didn't you check your messages? Were you working late?"

"No," she said, standing in front of him, legs apart, hands on hips. She hadn't bothered to comb her hair or repair her makeup, and she looked, she knew, like a woman who had been playing around. "I went out for a drink."

"With whom?" he asked, taking in her appearance now. A flush spread over his face. "What's going on?"

"I want you to fuck me in the ass, big boy," she said. "I want you to ram that big, hard dick in me and make me whimper."

"Amanda, what's going on with you?" he demanded.

"I said," she repeated more primly this time, "I want it now. Anal sex." She unzipped her black skirt. It fell to the floor, and she stepped out of it. She was wearing lace-topped thigh-highs in sheer black—she never wore panty hose—and black lace boy-cut briefs. Her cream-colored cashmere sweater clung to her heaving breasts. "Now," she said.

He followed her into the bedroom. She pulled off the sweater and panties, then got into the rear-entry position with her breasts pressed flat against the bed, ass raised. Her legs trembled slightly. She heard him take the lubricant and a condom from his night-stand drawer. They didn't do this very often. It always hurt in the beginning. Sometimes she really got into it, but she had to get past the pain first.

"Are you sure?" he asked, his voice shaky.

"Fuck me," she said, her breath already jagged. "Do it!"

She heard his pants hit the floor, felt the cool, wet slickness of the lubricant as he worked it into her anus with one, then two fingers. *Relax,* she told herself. *Relax those sphincter muscles.* Her heart was pounding in her chest. She felt erotic dread and longing deep in her belly. Eyes closed, she heard him open the condom package. And then he was behind her, his hands on her ass, parting her cheeks, the head of his sheathed penis probing. She pushed hard against him, gasping as he penetrated her asshole.

"Fuck me," she repeated before he could ask, *Did I hurt you? Should I go slowly?* "Fuck me," she gasped as he thrust into her, hard and deep, searing her. "Yes," she whimpered, "yes." She kept her eyes shut hard against tears.

He held on to her ass, pushing hard into her, pulling back so far that he was almost out, driving in again. She moved with him, through the pain, into a place she'd never been before, where the pleasure could be so intense only because there had been pain. They sounded like animals, gasping, heaving, panting in torment. She held one hand to her clitoris and pressed against it in time with his strokes. He claimed her, possessed her totally now. She felt the orgasm beginning deep inside her and bursting throughout her whole body.

And she was still coming in waves when he came deep inside her.

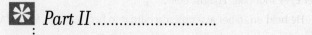

Part II

DESIRE

"I Want Sex; He Doesn't."

Increasingly he is the one saying, "Not tonight, honey."

Why are so many young (or relatively young) and physically able men turning down sex with their partners? Theories abound. It's the postfeminist male's passive/aggressive response to sexually assertive women. Or, confused by women's conflicting messages, needs, desires, and wants, he has lost his own capacity for rampant sexual desire. Or "giving her an orgasm" just takes too long. Or he says, "Not tonight, honey," because he's online, masturbating alone with his favorite porn.

"Porn is quick, and the path to the payoff is predictable, and women are none of the above," says a thirty-five-year-old married man who has sex alone in his home office two or three nights a week and only once a week in bed with his wife. "It's easier."

Whatever. If she wants more sex than he does, she has to take the lead in changing the status quo. Here are her options: Masturbate. Have an affair. Live with her frustrations. (Kickboxing is good for relieving pent-up sexual frustration.) Make whatever deal with him she has to make to get him into bed more often.

The women who used this Sex Life Makeover plan successfully just wanted more sex. They didn't campaign to end his porn use or engage him in a dialogue about the changing roles of men and women in twenty-first-century relationships. If "I want it—and I want it now" is your mantra, you *can* get it.

Can you resolve the gender-gap issues in seven days? No. Can they ever be resolved? Probably not.

The Standard Advice

The therapists say: Work out the conflicts between you. Examine his hidden issues relating to female sexuality. Get him into a treatment program for online sex addicts.

The sexperts say: Buy new lingerie. Flirt with him. Diet, exercise, get your hair done. Put your head on his shoulder and pretend to be interested in everything he says.

Lingerie is always good. Flirting is almost a lost art in America. We should lead the revival. Women in other places—Paris, for example—know how to make provocative eye contact: the kind of eye contact that expresses dirty thoughts in a ladylike way. First, there is the brief but intense glance, in which you instantly lock eyes with your partner for just a second or two and then quickly look away. Second is the eye flirt, during which you repeatedly look away and then back, a game of tease. Finally there's the eye embrace, a deep engagement that lasts longer than a few seconds. Use them all. And make love with your eyes open too.

I'm all in favor of flirting—but you need something a little stronger to jump-start that sex life tonight.

The Instant First-night Sex Life Makeover:
Unplug Him and Use Him

1. Coerce him into a shutdown agreement.

No online access for the evening—or at least until after he has pleasured you. Keep your negotiating language free of judgmental and pejorative terms. You can't accuse him of being a pervert one minute and ask him to satisfy your needs the next. Whatever you think about his taste in porn, put that aside. Keep the goal in mind: You want sex and you want it *now*.

If dirty talk excites him and you can pull it off comfortably, do that.

2. Accept no pleas of exhaustion, mental or physical.

This is a no-excuses demand-performance night. Ravish him. But let him know that he is under no obligation to have an orgasm or even to sustain an erection. It's all about you. When you're finished with him, he can roll over and go to sleep.

Games you can play with a semierect penis:

"STUFF" AND SPOON

In the spoon position (side by side or his front to your back), insert his semierect penis into your vagina. With fingers splayed downward, use one hand to hold the penis in place between your thumb and first finger, forming a V around the base, the flat of your palm caressing the shaft. Massage the perineum (the area between the base of testicles and the anus) with your fingertips. A perineum massage will give many men an erection. Use the other hand to stroke your clitoris. Maintain a slow but steady intercourse motion.

OR USE HIM TO MASTURBATE

Let him lie on his back. Straddle him and take his penis, flaccid or erect, in hand. Use the head to stroke and tease your clitoris. If he's hard enough, put him inside, then quickly take him out. Continue using the head of the penis to bring yourself to orgasm.

OR HAVE HIM MASTURBATE YOU

Ask him to hold you in his arms and bring you to orgasm manually. Suck his finger, bite his nipples, blow in his ear—whatever amuses you.

Rare is the man who will not rise to one of these occasions—especially when the performance pressure is off.

The continued success of this plan depends on your maintaining your key attitudes: no judgments about why he hasn't been meeting your needs in the recent past, and no excuses for him now. When you are single-minded in pursuit of pleasure from a man, you will get it.

1. Masturbate.

Watching you masturbate is probably high on his sex wish list. You, on the other hand, may touch yourself *discreetly* during intercourse because you assume he will feel threatened or hurt if he sees you helping yourself to an orgasm. For most men that's not true. They are aroused by catching your little theatrical flourish to the finish line. And they would love to catch an entire solo performance.

✳ Technique Tips

> *Don't ask him for sex. Don't tell him you want it. Show him. Put on a sexy shirt and nothing else (except maybe a pair of black thigh-high lace-trimmed stockings and a pair of heels; women should toss out panty hose and wear sensible heels for work only). Assume a provocative position with your back against the headboard, legs open and bent at the knees, ass elevated by a pillow or two. Place two fingers in an inverted V straddling your clitoris. That*

hand position is good for encouraging your orgasm—and also for showing him just what you've got.

Throw yourself into masturbation with abandon. If you have the kind of headboard that permits it, put one hand over your head and grasp a rung or bedpost. Thrust your pelvis forward. Pant and moan.

Add some flashy moves like:

The Figure Eight: Use one finger to glide up, over, and around your clitoris as if you were tracing the number eight.

The Two-finger Thrill: Hold two fingers parallel on either side of your clitoris. Run them up and down and then sideways.

And don't be shy about incorporating a vibrator into your solo sex play. It's a reliable way of reaching orgasm. And he may get some ideas on how to use the vibrator to pleasure you by watching. I don't suggest starting with the vibrator because finger play allows you to expose yourself rather than be hidden behind the hand wielding the implement. Seeing your fingers wet with your own moisture is a real turn-on.

2. Quickies!

Men love quickies: sex, including intercourse, in ten minutes or less. If you're trying to get him interested in having sex more often, suggest quickies. That eliminates his primary objection: Getting you aroused and then satisfying you can take so long. Yes, quickies can work for women too. Quickies have gotten a bad rap in the past as the "wham, bam, thank you, ma'am" method of doing it, but you're staging these quickies, and you will be prepared for them.

The keys to success: Do the foreplay on your own time. (Slip into the bathroom or bedroom alone and masturbate, but not to orgasm.) Position yourself during intercourse so that you get the maximum stimulation possible to your clitoris. And give yourself a helping hand to orgasm from the start. Don't wait to touch yourself until you're nearing orgasm.

Some quickie positions that really work:

❋ Technique Tips

THE NEW MISSIONARY

She lies on her back with her legs up as straight and high as they will comfortably go. He kneels in front of her. The position lengthens her vaginal barrel, creating a tighter feeling for him. The angle of penetration affords her greater friction—and she has her hands free to stimulate her clitoris at the same time.

THE SCINTILLATING SIDE BY SIDE

She is on her back with her inner leg (the one closer to him) on top of his legs and her outer leg between his legs. (Once you figure out how the legs stack up—like an X—the position is simple.) Her ass faces him, but she can also angle her body so that she turns her face toward him.

> *With hands free, he can use a vibrator or his fingers to stimulate her during intercourse.*
>
> STANDING AGAINST THE WALL
> *It looks hot in the movies because it is hot. She removes her panties; he unzips his trousers. He holds her to him tightly, with one or both hands around her ass. She has one leg wrapped around his waist. The friction is amazing.*

3. Get on top.

All he need provide is a modest erection. You can take care of the rest, including keeping that erection going. Men love the female-superior position, especially when they're tired, tipsy, or not that into sex. It's like giving them a free ride. Make the visuals outstanding—and give him a few surprises in your riding style.

❋Technique Tips

> THE CORKSCREW TWIST
> *Sit on top of him, insert him, and lean forward, lifting yourself three-quarters of the way up his penis. Put your hands on his shoulders for balance. Then move your pelvis to the right and push yourself down at the same time. Pull back up and then move your pelvis to the left as*

you push down again. Go back and forth like this until he can't remember his own name.

Once you get the hang of the twist, add a PC flex to the move. Tighten your PCs on the downward push; then relax them while coming back up.

Or, if you are flexible, do the twist while bending backward with your hands resting on his knees.

4. Submit.

Tell him you want to be submissive. You want him to take you the way Rhett undoubtedly took Scarlett. If he likes you in lingerie, that's what you'll be wearing. His fantasies run to French-maid's uniforms? Get a frilly white apron, cap, and tiny black dress. Be prepared to surrender to his desires.

It's all about him this time. Take-no-prisoners sex is good for a man's ego. It fuels his fantasies. And thus it achieves your goal: He will want to have sex more often.

5. Give *him* a G-spot orgasm.

If you want to get a man more interested in sex—the kind of sex he can't have alone, penis in one hand, mouse in the other—you may need to go some places you haven't gone before, like his perineum, the area rich in nerve endings between the base of the testicles and the anus. Stroke it, tickle it, massage it with your thumb. Add a little caressing, even licking of the rim of his anus if you're both comfortable with that.

Pay attention to the subtle signs that he is close to the point of ejaculation. Some men hold their breath. Others breathe with more intensity. He might make a certain sound—or get suddenly quiet. Every man does something in exactly the same way before every orgasm. (And this is never the time to say: "No, not yet!" or "Wait!" No matter where you are in your process, let him have his five seconds of bliss and take care of you later.)

Now: Stimulate his secret G-spot. Use your thumb or finger to exert firm but gentle pressure on his perineum. (If he is comfortable with it, insert a well-lubricated finger into his anus and stimulate the G-spot from the inside.) That will trigger an orgasm that he feels in his genitals, anus, and radiating throughout his pelvis and buttocks.

What Sex Life Makeover Participants Say

"In the past I approached my husband about sex by saying, 'We need to talk.' That is just the worst way to get laid. Never works."

"We experienced an amazing turn-around—which I attribute to 1. Masturbating for him and 2. Discovering his perineum. I'd read about the P-spot in sex advice articles, but never gone for it. Should have done that years ago."

"I really do think his online porn is disgusting and pathetic. But I have a new motto: Shut up and suck if you want to be sucked."

❊ Beauty Awakens Her Man

"Aren't men supposed to be the sex always trying to get some?" Karla teased James.

"Take your tongue out of my ear," he said, gently pushing her face away from him. "That tickles."

James was always too tired or too involved in watching a game or too busy working on one of their many renovation projects. Sometimes she was jealous of their Victorian home. *"She,"* she complained to friends, because she thought of the house as a female entity, "gets more attention than I do." Karla had tried the tricks: dressing in heels, bra, and panties and standing in front of the television set; vacuuming in one of his shirts and nothing else; leaving seductive messages on his voice mail and notes in his pocket. They rarely worked. And she was horny most of the time!

"I am a woman who wants it seven days a week, married to a man who is happy with once or twice," she lamented.

And then the solution came to her while she was masturbating to a video alone in their bed: She would awaken him the way the Prince awakened Sleeping Beauty.

That night after he fell asleep, she slid her hand under the sheet and caressed his penis. Gently she held his flaccid organ in her hand, imagining it as it would be soon: erect, standing straight out from his body like a soldier on guard duty. She ran her thumb in circles around the head and played long finger strokes up and down the shaft. His penis trembled in her hand, coming to life slowly in awkward jolts like a newborn colt standing for the first time.

When he was firm, she let him go, rolled over, and went to sleep.

In the morning he held her a little longer than usual in their good-bye hug before they both hurried off to their jobs. "Have a good day!" he called after her. Was there a wistful note in his voice, a hint of "longing" in his eye?

The next night after he fell asleep, she took his penis in hand once again. This time it sprang to life almost instantly, as if it had been lying in wait for her. She rolled over on her side close to him and rubbed his penis between the palms of her hands. He was, she told herself, a stick, and she was making fire. A small moan escaped his lips.

She let him go, rolled over, and went to sleep.

In the morning when she kissed him good-bye, she blew lightly in his ear. He held on to her. "Put your tongue in my ear," he said. "That feels good." But she told him she didn't have time.

On the third night, his penis was already stiff when she reached for it. She lifted the sheet and saw it proud and beautiful like a piece of pink marble elegantly carved. Carefully she turned back the sheet, took the base of his penis firmly in hand, wet her lips, and put him in her mouth. His body trembled in response. She swirled her tongue around the head of his penis, then sucked lightly. Several long strokes of her tongue down the shaft, then back to the head.

"Oh," he said, and she felt his body waking.

She rolled over, closed her eyes, and pretended to be asleep.

"Karla," he whispered. He rolled toward her, wrapped an arm around her. She felt his erection pushing hopefully against her ass. And she wanted to reach around, grasp him, and put him inside her aching pussy. "Karla, are you asleep?" he asked softly.

"Um," she said, lifting his arm and moving away from him before he could feel her pounding heart. "Night, baby."

In the morning, he said, "I had a dream last night. You were giving me head."

"Really?" she asked, feigning uninterest. "No time to talk this morning, honey. I have an early meeting!"

That afternoon, because she knew he would finally want sex when she came home, she called to tell him she had to work late. "And don't wait up . . . I'm meeting girlfriends for margaritas later."

He was disappointed—not that his disappointment soothed the ache in her groin.

That night she slid under the sheets. Asleep, he was naked and warm, his erection waving to her. She put her hand around his penis and suppressed a sigh. His hand covered hers.

"You're not rolling over," he said. "I want you."

In one smooth move, he lifted her up on top of him. She sobbed in happiness and relief as she felt him swell even bigger inside her. Leaning over him so that her nipples grazed his as she rode him, she licked his ear. He moaned and didn't pull away from her tongue.

"He Wants Sex; I Don't."

What is more pathetic than a man begging and pleading for sex?

"I am so contemptuous of my husband when he starts whining for sex that I feel like it's a pity fuck even if I'm into it," a twenty-nine-year-old wife of four years told me. She sighed as she added, "It's just not manly. I would be thrilled if he occasionally threw me down on the bed and said, 'I want you and I will have you now.'"

The partner who wants less sex typically feels guilty—and like something of an erotic failure. On the one hand, being hounded for sex is annoying and leads you to cast the other in the role of satyr or nympho. On the other hand, you secretly fear that there is something wrong with you because you don't want sex very often.

The bottom line for her: Unless you want him to look

elsewhere, you need to accommodate his desires. By removing the fights/debates over frequency, you can focus on
more important issues, like how, not how often. Stop using
"no" as your fallback position.

The bottom line for him: You must not be driving her
wild in bed or she wouldn't be pushing you away so much of
the time. If you want more sex, make the sex better for her.
Stop begging and start seducing.

The Standard Advice

The experts tell him: Be more romantic. Bring flowers,
make dates, hold her hand in public.

And the experts tell her: Communicate with him. Tell
him what you need and want in bed. Give in occasionally
and just do it anyway.

"Just do it" is always good advice, whether she's the one
with less interest or he is or neither of them can work up
much enthusiasm for sex—and they should "just do it" more
than occasionally. The more you "do it," the less pressure
you put on each other to perform. Every lovemaking event
need not be a memorable one.

Remember: "Okay sex" with a regular partner is better
than no sex at all. If you're in a marriage or committed
monogamous relationship, having frequent sex helps you
deal more effectively with all the little irritants in the relationship, in life itself. Sex takes the edge off, at least tem-
porarily.

He should bring flowers frequently whether he wants sex

or not. We all need more romance in our lives. But romance isn't enough to turn around your sex life tonight.

The Instant First-night Makeover: It's All about Her

What is the sexiest thing a man can do for a woman?

A lot of women say: Take charge of dinner and/or kitchen cleanup *and* put the kids to bed. You may have to take on more of the domestic chores and child care to get her in the mood. While you're scraping the macaroni and cheese off the kitchen table, send her to a bubble bath. Afterward give her a special gift: a G-spot vibrator.

Say, "Tonight, honey, I want to please you. Never mind me."

And really impress her by finding that G-spot—and for extra credit, her AFE zone!—with your fingers before you turn on the toy.

❋ Technique Tips

The G-spot is a mass of spongy tissue located in the front wall of the vagina halfway between the pubic bone and the cervix and below the opening of the urethra. When stimulated, it swells. Some women ejaculate a clear, odorless fluid when their G-spots are highly stimulated.

The AFE zone is a small, sensitive patch of textured skin on the top of the vagina, closer to the cervix.

Have her lie down. With the palm of your hand facing

you, insert a well-lubricated finger or two into her vagina. Explore the front wall. You'll know you've found the AFE zone when she begins lubricating. Stroking that sensitive zone makes most women lubricate immediately. When you feel the G-spot, stimulate it by making a "come hither" motion toward her navel. Most women become aroused by this stroking movement.

When she is ready, replace your fingers with the G-spot vibrator. She should reach orgasm fairly quickly. You will have an erection just watching. And she will probably be so grateful that she wants to play with it.

The Sex Life Makeover Plan

1. Masturbate.

Okay, women are not as enthusiastic about watching their partners masturbate as men are. But she might surprise you by expressing interest when you say, "Honey, do you mind if I come?" after you've held her and kissed her—and obviously become aroused. Some women do like to watch. If she's not one of them, she should be the person to leave the room or look the other way. Don't hide from her.

For many husbands, masturbation is the dirty little secret. Bring it out into the open and see what happens. Ask her if you can use her vibrator. Surely that will get her attention.

✳ Technique Tips

ELECTRIC MASTURBATION, HIS

Start on low speed. Run the vibrator along the shaft, then press it against the base, the scrotum, and the perineum. Experiment with higher speeds and firmer pressures. You can have a stronger climax by resisting the urge to grasp your penis and perform manual masturbation. Used correctly, the vibrator takes longer for men—while it's typically the opposite for women.

2. Shamelessly make sex deals and compromises.

Maybe arousing her and bringing her to orgasm really does "take too long." You want more sex, don't you? Find the time to do it her way.

✳ Technique Tips

The surest, quickest route to her arousal is your fingers applied to her G-spot and AFE zone [see page 42 for directions.] But in doing that, you can look like—and make her feel like you are—a gynecologist performing an exam. The illustrations in some popular sex guides only reinforce that image of the dispassionate explorer taking on the vagina in his pursuit of personal pleasure.

To pull this move off when you are the one wanting more sex, you need to make it look like you are passionately diving into her, not clinically turning her on to get to your goal. Breathe heavily. Moan. Let your fingers express avid desire.

And don't go straight for the spots. Linger lovingly in her intimate zone like an acolyte in prayer. Then go for it.

3. Bribe her. Offer to do her chores in exchange for a blow job. Supervise the homework, run the soccer car pool—what would you do for a quickie? Make that woman some offers she can't refuse.

If there's something she doesn't like to do—anal sex, intercourse in the doggy position—don't bring it up this week. Maybe not next week either. Give it a rest. I'm not saying you'll never get this. I'm saying: Getting it at all is your first priority now. Making her comfortable, both mentally and physically, is essential. And no one is comfortable when they're being pushed to do something they don't want to do.

4. Learn new tricks.

Men are not the gender that buys sex books and magazines filled with sex advice articles. They are the gender that thinks they know what they're doing in bed anyway. Get over yourself. We can all learn new tricks.

THE SEDUCTIVE KISS

Cradle her face in your hands. Caress her with your eyes. Go in for the kiss tenderly. As your kiss progresses, cradle her head and neck with your hands.

Lean her against a wall or a door. Take her hands and hold them over her head against the wall or door as you're kissing her, exploring her lips, tongue, and mouth with the tip of your tongue and your own lips. Never push your whole tongue into her mouth. That is not a French kiss. It is a tongue sandwich.

Nuzzle her. Bury your nose in her neck, her cleavage.

Come back to the kiss. Take her face into your hands again. Kiss her until you feel her melting into your body. Then just hold her. See where she takes it from there.

THE AROUSING TOUCH

Touch her in places you don't normally touch her. Stroke her neck with one finger. Play with the ends of her hair. If she has long hair, lift it off her neck and kiss her neck. If she has short hair, run a finger through the hairs at the base of her neck as if you were ruffling them.

When her head is resting on your shoulder, massage her scalp lightly with your knuckles or finger pads.

Hold her hand. You stopped doing that a while ago, right? Caress her hand with your thumb.

Hold her wrist, keeping your thumb on her pulse.

Lick her belly button.

Stroke her back in long, broad strokes. Unless she is ex-tremely ticklish, run your fingers up her sides. Bite her shoulders—lightly, of course.

Massage her calves.

Ask for her help. Put her hand over yours and ask her to show you how she likes to be touched.

EROTIC STROKES

The spider's legs is a highly arousing light touch. Use the pads of your fingers as if they were spider's legs wan-dering up and down her body. The touch is light, teasing. It makes no demands.

In the walk of love, you walk your fingers around her body from one erogenous zone to another. Moving more slowly and applying a little more pressure than in spi-der's legs, you are creating highly charged electric path-ways as you go. She will be aroused.

The nipple stroke uses the palm of your hand to brush lightly over her nipples. Gently rub her nipples between your fingers. Squeeze. Push them into her breasts, then gently pull them out, perhaps lightly twisting at the same time. Blow over her nipples wetted with your saliva.

(Women can use these erotic touches on men too.)

BODY WORSHIP

Women complain that their husbands or longtime lovers touch them in the same ways all the time. The familiar

> *foreplay pattern feels like something you're doing to get her to the goal. She resents that.*
>
> *When you're holding and kissing her, let your hands roam her body as though she were a treasure you're being allowed to fondle. Stop kissing, step back from her, take her hands in yours, and frankly admire her body. Focus on the parts you love. If she has nice breasts, worship them with your eyes.*
>
> *Once you're naked together, worship her with your tongue, your lips, your hands. Circle her nipples with your tongue. Make long, slow strokes with your tongue up from the backs of her knees to her genitals. Don't rush. By the time you start performing cunnilingus, she should be moaning softly and lifting her pelvis to greet you.*

5. Make out.

Women love to make out—all that kissing, caressing, stroking, and petting without intercourse. Men quit making out as soon as they have moved her into the intercourse phase. And that's a shame. Making out is pure play. It's arousing. Even if makeout games don't lead to sex tonight, she'll be more willing tomorrow. Try doing "everything but" one night and see what happens. One or both of you might have an orgasm in your pants—just like high school.

BUMP AND GRIND

Standing fully dressed, kiss and caress each other with your pelvises pressed together. When you feel the steam rising between the two of you, she bumps into him on the upstroke and grinds into him on the downstroke. Wrap one leg around his waist or use a door or wall for balance—but don't lie down.

OUTERCOURSE

Do this on the floor, the sofa, or even in the bathroom. You can remove or unbutton shirts, but the pants stay on. Tease and stroke each other's genitals through the clothes. Lick, kiss, nibble above the waist. Get into an intercourse position, either one on top, and simulate the action. Move fast and hard. See if you can stop before orgasm.

6. Submit.

Male sexual submission is a thrilling concept for many women. Maybe she's fantasized tying you to the bedposts, spanking you, and sitting on your face. She might like you down on your knees, licking her from her instep arched high in stilettos all the way up to her clitoris. Beg her to dominate you. Unleash the sexually assertive woman in her.

"I had pushed for sex so hard and so long that I'd pushed us both into opposing corners. This week did turn around our sex life. I learned how to be a better lover. And I don't know why it didn't occur to me a few years ago that I needed to turn up the heat in the bedroom."

"Here's the relationship conundrum: On the one hand you are entitled to sex with this person. On the other hand, entitlement sex gets boring. And some people, like my girl, don't like handing out entitlements. Change is good. We needed the change."

✳ Desire

Desire can feel so overwhelming and acute that the memory of it outlasts even the memory of the lovemaking. And that's how it was for Jocelyn. She could recall the moment when she wanted him, a moment that existed with no ties to the future or the past. The imprint of that intense longing on her senses was, she sometimes thought, all that remained of her desire for her husband.

She closed her eyes and saw him still there. Running one hand languidly through the water, he was down on his haunches in an oversize marble tub. They had spent the night together in a luxury hotel suite in a city roughly equidistant between the ones in which they were living then. That morning they were headed in opposite geographical directions and, she feared, headed out of each other's emotional orbits too.

From the doorway where she leaned against the wall adjusting the strap on a sling-back high-heeled pump, she watched him stir the water in the tub and felt his long fingers probing, circling, stirring inside her.

His biceps swelled and contracted slightly as his arm moved, the action pumping desire throughout her body. His penis, half-erect, hung down but away from his body. She felt sexual hunger for him throughout her body, even on the surface of her skin.

He looked up, and she turned away because she didn't want him to read what she wanted in her eyes. "I guess you're happy," he said, but she couldn't remember what it was he thought was making her happy. Their leave-taking?

Nor could she remember why on that particular morning the end of their relationship seemed both clear and unfathomable—when in fact, it didn't end there at all.

All she could remember was wanting him inside her, wanting his mouth and his hands, wanting his touch and his taste and his scent. She didn't remember feeling happy. Or sad. *The words simply don't,* she thought, *apply to desire.*

She stood there standing fully clothed in a crisp linen suit while he hunkered down, calmly distributing a thin stream of cold water into the overheated tub, steam like primordial mist licking his testicles as desire, a swift, hot sword, sliced through her body. And she waited for him to look at her with that depth of wanting in his hooded eyes. But he didn't look up.

"What are you thinking about so hard?" he asked her.

"I was thinking about how we were," she said.

He laughed and she walked away from him out onto the sun porch. Her African violets were huge and lush in the winter sun.

She remembered the first time they'd made love. At the point of his orgasm, he said, "I want you again."

He slid one hand between their bodies and held himself inside her. It was important to him that he not fall out. She tensed her muscles around him. He covered her mouth with his and fed her his soft moans and whimpers. His body performed feats that day they could not have reasonably expected of it.

His passion finally exhausted both of them, but his hunger was not satisfied. Throughout the night, he slept fitfully, his hands grasping parts of her flesh, seeking places he might enter. They had been lovers for less than two weeks when her desire matched his own.

They had gone to dinner at the home of his good friends. In those early days, she was listening closely to his conversation with others for clues to him, eager to learn who he was and jealous because they knew and she didn't. He went into the kitchen to open a bottle of wine with one of those old-fashioned corkscrews. From the sofa in the living room, she saw his gold watch catch the light as he twisted the bottle, gently pulling it away from the cork. She wanted to press her mouth against his wrist and feel his pulse on her lips. The wall of her vagina began to sweat, then swell. Everything in the space between them ceased to exist.

Jocelyn was consumed with desire for him. They began making love in the cab on the way back to her apartment. At one point, her mouth surrounding his penis, she wanted from him what men fear women want from them: everything. She wanted to suck him dry and yet have him hard and pulsating inside her at the same time.

Now she remembered the moment of first longing as if it were etched on her body. Sometimes when she masturbated, she felt

those sense memories being awakened as her hands traced the secret markings she imagined desire for him had left on her.

"Are you still thinking about us?" he asked from the doorway.

She looked up into his hooded eyes and suddenly she tasted his
semen in her mouth. "Are you still thinking about us?" he repeated, his voice thick and heavy. His voice quavered. Her hands
trembled.

Jocelyn longed for him, her whole being centered once again in
her vulva, the need so great.

"We Don't Have the Time— or the Energy—for Sex."

In November 2004 *Parenting* magazine published a survey in which 43 percent of young mothers said their sex lives were routine, while 30 percent rated them virtually nonexistent. Fifty-nine percent said they would like to have sex twice a week, while only 37 percent said they did. There were three primary excuses for why the sex just wasn't happening: too tired, no time, and can't shut off the mental to-do list.

The no-time, no-energy couples are everywhere.

The Standard Advice

The experts say: Plan weekend getaways. Set the alarm to make love after a few hours' sleep. Do it in the morning when his testosterone level is naturally highest.

The advice ignores the obvious: No time for weekend getaways, or at least not very often. And who wants to have sex only when they can go on vacation? They're already only getting a few hours' sleep a night, which makes waking up midway problematic, though not impossible. And there may be enough time for brief erotic touch in the mornings, but not much else.

Dr. Carole Pasahow developed a treatment plan for no-time, no-energy couples, the 21-Day Passion Fix (as outlined in her book, *Sexy Encounters: 21 Days of Provocative Passion Fixes*). It's a good book because it teaches people how to use fantasies to enrich their sex lives. Check it out. But you need to get something done tonight.

The Instant First-night Makeover: Hand Jobs

Sex begets more sex. The too-tired, too-busy couple are not in a sexual rut. They're out of the sexual habit. The problem with that: Sex begins to seem like an event, a holiday, an out-of-the-ordinary experience. You need to put sex back into your daily lives—tonight.

You may be tired and time-pressured, but you will end up lying side by side at the end of the day. In that position, you can give one another a hand. Yes, that counts as "sex."

THE ULTIMATE HAND JOB

Like he's never had before and couldn't possibly give himself.

Clasp your lubricated hands together, fingers interlaced, snugly around the shaft of his penis. Move your hands up the shaft in one long twisting motion. Repeat the move back down the shaft. Now vary that move by eliminating the twist.

When he has a firm erection, clasp your hands at the top of the shaft. Gently contract and release them around the shaft at approximately one-second intervals. Keep doing this up and down the shaft, stopping at the rim where the shaft meets the head.

Alternate the twisting and contracting strokes until he is ready to ejaculate. Then hold him firmly in both hands, gently contracting them in time with his spasms. Finish him off by running your thumb from the base of the shaft on the underside up to the head.

GIVE HER A HAND

Rub lubricant into your hands. Using a firm but not hard upward stroke with the palm of your hand, start caressing her inner thighs using your palms alone. Work your way toward her genitals with that same stroke. Gently part her lips with your fingers. Then stroke her inner lips.

Be sure your thumb and forefinger are well lubricated.

Use them to surround her clitoris. Massage. Some women like to have their clitoris stroked directly. If she does, take her clitoris between thumb and forefinger and gently rotate.

Hold two fingers in the shape of a V and put them around her clitoris. Press down lightly. Pull back. Press down again and back up. This creates a rocking motion that may bring her to orgasm. If not, alternate the circular move around the clitoris, the rotating move (if she likes direct stimulation), and the rocking V until she does reach orgasm.

The Sex Life Makeover Plan

1. Foreplay in the morning; release at night.

Stroking and caressing are open-ended pleasures in some cultures. In the West, particularly America, they are steps to the goal: intercourse. Forget the end for the moment and concentrate on the means. Think of erotic contact as play. Arouse each other in the morning through French kisses and genital caresses. Sex will be on your mind that day—making it much more likely you'll find the time and energy for it before bedtime.

2. Go to sleep in the stuffing-and-spooning position.

Insert his flaccid penis and fall asleep together in the spoon position. Maybe his erection will awaken both of you.

Even if there is no middle-of-the-night booty call and you wake up separate, not entangled, you will feel more erotically inclined toward each other. The idea of sex has been placed in your minds.

3. Do it sitting down.

Have sex in a chair. She can straddle him face-to-face, her legs brought up to the sides in an overstuffed chair or feet on the floor on either side of a straight-backed chair. Or she can face outward, allowing him more freedom to reach around her body and play with her breasts and clitoris.

Or the bathtub. Facing the faucet, she kneels in a tub half-filled with warm water. Holding the sides of the tub, she leans forward. He enters from behind. Either of them can use a handheld showerhead to direct water onto her clitoris.

Or sit facing each other in bed, both supported by stacks of pillows at the back. She opens her legs and he strokes her clitoris with the underside of his penis. He doesn't need a firm erection for this position.

4. Modify intercourse positions—for maximum comfort and intimacy.

You may not be familiar with the basic sitting position (called the Yab-Yum in Tantric sex), but it's good for prolonging the man's arousal—or taking advantage of the fact that he is only somewhat aroused.

Sit in the center of the bed facing each other. Wrap your legs around each other so you're sitting on his legs. Place your right hands at the back of each other's neck, your left hands on each other's tailbones. Place his penis inside her so it exerts as much indirect pressure as possible on her clitoris.

Rock slowly together while rubbing each other's back and maintaining deep eye contact. She can make the position hotter for her by sitting on one more pillows so her G-spot and clitoris receive more stimulation. This is the best intercourse position for combining emotional closeness—which couples who haven't been making love regularly need—and physical satisfaction.

5. Shower together—or at least run the shower while you have a quickie standing up in the bathroom.

Once children are old enough to be left alone in a room with their toys and/or a video, you can close the bathroom door and do this on a weekend morning or an early evening.

Another alternative: Take turns being the partner who is satisfied in these spontaneous encounters if you are both afraid to let go while the kids are alone outside the door.

ULTIMATE FELLATIO

Swallowing is not difficult—and he will love you for doing it. Follow the fellatio instructions on page 121. If you're worried that he will thrust too deeply and gag you when he's near orgasm, use your thumb and forefinger to form a ring—an okay sign—around your mouth. You can control the timing of his ejaculation by using a press-release-press motion with your finger pad or thumb on his perineum when you are ready for him to release.

You can also perform the showy "deep throat" move in the bedroom by simply lying on your back with your head off the bed. The mouth and throat will form a smooth line. His ejaculate will go straight down your throat.

6. Just do it.

Having sex can be like riding an exercise bike. You think you can't possibly get into the saddle today, but you do, and suddenly you're not tired anymore. In fact, you're exhilarated. Sometimes having sex when you think you're too tired and stressed is the best thing you can do.

Practice competitive sex, if that motivates you. Therapists say we shouldn't worry about how much sex our friends and neighbors are having. Well, why not be inspired to have better sex lives because we want to keep up with the Joneses? Initiate sex talks with friends for the specific reason of finding out what they're doing—and how often they're doing it. Read sex surveys in magazines. Go for the gold.

What Sex Life Makeover Participants Say

"Women tend to downplay the importance of good, hot, steamy, down-and-dirty sex in keeping couples together. I was one of those women. I'm not anymore."

" 'Just do it' is the best advice anyone ever gave me about sex."

"Tension and stress make you tired. Orgasms relieve that. Have sex when you're too tired to have sex and you're less tired. It's a miracle!"

The Orgasm Loop

I developed this technique for female orgasm by combining Western cognitive psychology with Eastern erotic and martial-arts techniques. It's a virtually no-fail orgasm technique for women. Whether you have trouble reaching orgasm regularly during lovemaking or want to experience more intense or multiple orgasms, the Orgasm Loop will take you there.

I couldn't decide where in the chapters to drop this sidebar because, like Kegel exercises, it is an important element in every makeover. Why here then? The third element that keeps no-time, no-energy women in the no-sex column is difficulty in shutting down the part of their brains that keeps going back to the to-do list. They just can't stop concentrating on everything else, clear their minds, and surrender to desire and arousal.

The Orgasm Loop overcomes that significant obstacle.

In women the mind-body connection is not as obvious as it is in men. We don't see our arousal—so we need to visualize it. Recent studies have strengthened the conclusion most of us have already drawn about women and sex: So much of it is in the head. If she doesn't get her head into sex, it never really happens for her.

Men are sexually simple; women are not. He gets an erection and he knows he wants to have sex. The male erection-brain connection is strong. A woman's genitals don't always get the message to her brain—in part because the signs of female arousal are more subtle. Often she has sex without fully tapping into her arousal—making orgasm problematic. Or she allows herself to become distracted by body issues, performance concerns, stress, tension, worry—and loses her arousal, at least for a time, again making orgasm problematic.

WHAT IT IS

The Orgasm Loop is a revolutionary technique that fuses cognitive feedback research on female orgasm with Tantric breathing, and an adaptation of the same energy-focusing technique that allows martial-arts black belts to smash boards, bricks, and blocks.

WHY IT WORKS

The Orgasm Loop teaches a woman how to visualize her arousal and then focus all her sexual energy on achieving orgasm in a three-stage process.

The more she visualizes arousal, the more aroused she becomes—until orgasm is easy, as inevitable as it is for a man.

HOW IT WORKS

The three stages are: mental arousal; energy focus; physical moves, including breathing, PC flexing, and clitoral stimulation via hand, mouth, vibrator, or penis.

MENTAL AROUSAL

Close your eyes, clear your mind of distractions, and visualize your arousal.

Some women may visualize their genitalia—lips swelling, moisture forming, the color changing to a deeper pink. Other women may visualize a flower, perhaps an orchid. (The sensual flower photography of Georgia O'Keeffe can be an inspiration.) Some women may see arousal as a color; perhaps pink or red—or saffron yellow, the color of the goddess in Hindu mythology. Arousal can be a scene, like the beach at sunset.

Find the image that represents arousal to you and focus on it every time you use the Orgasm Loop. Focus to the extent that no other image enters your mind.

Note: Eye contact with your lover during the cognitive-conditioning phase will slow the process. Keep eyes closed during kissing/foreplay.

ENERGY FOCUS

When you are conscious of nothing but arousal, turn your focus inward.

Focus on a spot just below your navel (the inner chi, if we want to get technical). Breathe deeply and slowly and imagine that little spot of energy glowing and growing. Move it down into your genitals with your mental focus.

Hold that energy in place.

Now imagine a fiery coil of sexual energy located at the base of your spine (kundalini, or sexual energy). Uncoil it and move it into your genitals. Feel the undulating, coiling energy circling around and through the spot of glowing energy.

You have moved your body's energy into your genitals, particularly the clitoris. And you are experiencing heightened sensitivity to touch now, in part because your temperature increases with arousal. As your body feels warmer, you feel more alive, more sensuous.

Why these two spots?

The chi and the base of the spine where the kundalini energy is coiled are near the genitals, giving them both physical and psychological significance. You are bringing sexual heat to bear on the genitals from more than one direction. When you imagine holding the energy in these

two places, you are increasing the blood flow to those areas simply by using the power of the mind. Psychology in-
fluences physiology.

PHYSICAL MOVES

1. While maintaining your energy focus, use
breathing to intensify the mind-genital connection.
Imagine you are breathing fire in a circle, inhaling it
up from your genitals throughout your body and exhaling out your mouth. . . . Keep doing this in circular
fashion. (See pages 143–44 for more detailed instructions on fire breathing.)

The principle behind the circle of fire is a simple
one. The combination of controlled breathing and energy focusing creates heat. You literally move that heat
in and out of your body as you fire-breathe. Like any
form of deep breathing, fire breathing increases the
oxygen level in the blood. And it forces more blood into
your genital area.

2. Once you have created a circle of fire, flex your PC
muscles in time with your breathing. Tighten them as
you breathe in; loosen as you breathe out.

3. Apply clitoral stimulation—either orally or manually or by positioning yourself in intercourse to make
the hot-spot connection between the shaft of the penis
and the clitoris. Very little stimulation will be necessary at this point to achieve orgasm.

4. Keep up the fire breathing during intercourse.

Don't worry if you lose a cycle or two. Just pick it up again, especially at the point of orgasm because fire breathing intensifies orgasm.

And you can have more orgasms simply by maintaining the focus and the breathing instead or relaxing after the orgasm. When you feel yourself letting go after orgasm, focus on the arousal image again. Repeat the breathing and PC flexing. Think of the Orgasm Loop as your own film strip that you can keep running until you're exhausted.

WHAT WOMEN SAY ABOUT THE ORGASM LOOP

"I didn't think I 'needed' an orgasm technique because I usually had orgasms, but I was game to try. The first few times I couldn't get it all working together, the breathing, focusing, and the PC muscles. But then it did come together—and wow! I had a much stronger orgasm than normal. Now I use it all the time."

"Everything had to be 'right' for me to have an orgasm—and as my husband kept pointing out, everything was seldom 'right.' I needed to be relaxed and not stressed and have plenty of foreplay. Using the loop, I can have an orgasm anytime. In fact, I can have more than one—and it doesn't require him spending an hour warming me up. I practiced the loop a few times on my own before trying it with him—so he was shocked."

"I always felt like the sex started without me. I was

present in body only. That's why I had trouble reaching orgasm. So I was surprised at how easily and quickly I could make the loop work for me. Maybe I was always more aroused than I knew I was. Now I initiate lovemaking more often than he does—and he loves it. I just think about sex more often than I did."

✳ The Nooner

Andrea's Daytimer, November 5: Office visit with Dr. Steve, noon.

From Andrea's diary, Friday, November 5:

I walked into his office, into his arms, and we did not talk. He lifted the hair away from my face and kissed my forehead, my eyelids, my cheeks, and finally my mouth. Teasing me at first by lightly licking and sucking each lip, he finally thrust his tongue into my mouth at the same time he parted my legs with his thigh. I felt his erection inside those beautifully tailored Italian slacks. I wrapped one leg around his thigh, my heat enveloping his. As his tongue explored my mouth, I anticipated his penis inside me.

"We only have forty-five minutes," he murmured. He led me to the leather couch, which he'd covered with a blanket. "I want more," he said.

We stripped naked in seconds, my suit entangled with his on the chair where we'd tossed them. Lying side by side, we touched each other with healing strokes. I ran my hand along the curve of his hip and, cupping his buttock, drew him even closer to me. He lowered his head to my breast and took the nipple in his mouth. I cradled his head while he sucked me and thought of how it would feel when in seconds he put his mouth to my vagina. Shivering in anticipation, I reached for his penis and squeezed it gently.

"Make me come," I begged. "I can't wait."

I was thick and wet from wanting him. Without taking his mouth from my breast, he put his hand between my legs, his fingers sliding back and forth, in and out of me, while his thumb massaged my clitoris. The orgasm that began almost immediately was so strong it seemed to suck his fingers inside me. I came around his hand, the spasms shaking my whole body.

"You are so incredible," he said, but I could not speak. I buried my face in his chest, inhaling his scent. Crazy, but I was still hungry for him. "I want you now," he said.

He was on top of me then, holding my ass firmly with one hand and guiding that magnificent erection inside me with the other.

"Hard," I said. "I want you inside me as far as you can go."

My urgency released his passion, which became as insistent as my own. Growling deep in his throat, he lifted me off the couch in an act of penetration so deep and so total that I lost awareness of everything except his penis thrusting repeatedly inside me, claiming me, owning me. I came over and over again. When he ejaculated, I almost lost consciousness.

"I love you," he whispered. "I didn't hurt you, did I?"

"No, God, no, you were wonderful. I wanted you so much."

He held me tight against his chest, the hairs matted with our sweat. We stayed that way, without speaking, for a few minutes until we'd stopped panting. Then he laid me back against the sofa cushions, fluffing them before he put my head down, and stroked my labia until I was writhing, my hands over my head, grasping the arm of the sofa.

"I want to eat you out," he said huskily.

"Please," I begged.

And he lowered his mouth to my body as if he were about to partake of a sacrament.

Andrea's Daytimer, November 5: Drinks with boss, 5 P.M., discuss Carter case. Steve picks up baby at day care. Buy flowers on way home.

Part III

AROUSAL

"His/Her Body Doesn't Turn Me on Anymore."

Your partner has gained a significant amount of weight, gone soft, bald, soggy—or all that and more. While many couples continue to desire each other through the extra pounds and broken veins, some of us have trouble with that. Our desire and arousal are more dependent than average on the visual elements. Maybe we have a real dislike for fat. We didn't get fat, and we didn't expect the man/woman we married to gain a significant amount of weight either.

Expressing that feeling may be politically incorrect. But desire and arousal are dependent on how we are, not how we would like to be or society thinks that we should be. An affair or a divorce may or may not be an option. You wouldn't be reading this chapter if you didn't want to fix the sex with the person you love but no longer desire. If you are that person no longer desired, you have to get over your hurt

····

feelings and look at the situation objectively. Is it fair to expect your partner to pant after you no matter how you look, or how much you've let it all hang out?

This is the toughest Sex Life Makeover in the book. You *can*, however, pull it off.

The Standard Advice

The experts say: Get couples therapy—because fat is a relationship issue. Join a gym together. Take a spa vacation.

These are not bad ideas—especially joining a gym together. (Fat *can* be a relationship issue—a way of suppressing sexuality or getting even with the other.) Exercise boosts endorphins and makes everyone feel and eventually look sexier, more filled with verve and energy. Why don't you shake hands on that gym membership, or plan to walk daily, or buy a major piece of exercise equipment, like a stationary bike or rowing machine?

But you don't have to wait for an improved body. You can have good sex tonight.

The Instant First-night Makeover: Blindfolded Sex

Work with me here: Close your eyes and imagine your lover as she/he was when she/he did arouse you. Keep that image firmly in your mind. His voice hasn't changed tenor. Her touch is the same. Now put on a satin blindfold and let your lover pleasure you. If touching him or her spoils the fantasy—those rolls of flesh!—then don't touch. Just allow yourself to be touched.

And if you are the partner in charge of the pleasure, use your voice and touch to arouse. Talk about what you're going to do to him or her before you do it. Recall erotic highlights from your past together. Use the mouth and hand moves that once worked so well.

✳ Technique Tips

TIE AND TEASE

Get into a comfortable position. For most people, that's sitting up in bed with back against the headboard, arms outstretched to the sides, wrists lightly fastened to the headboard.

Use gentle restraints like Velcro handcuffs or loosely tied silk scarves or ties. Don't use metal handcuffs or tight knots. The bound person should be able to work his or her hands loose. It's a game, not an arrest.

Tease your partner with light kisses and touches. Use oils and lotions. Run a feather lightly up and down his or her inner thighs. Fondle nipples through a silk scarf. Put rose petals on your finger pads and massage your lover's genitals. Be creative in your use of sensual materials.

Vary the pattern of teasing strokes, from passionate kisses now to gentle caresses again.

Focus on the pleasure points: nipples, on both men and women; inner thighs; backs of knees; the neck; ears;

> *the line from the navel down to the pubis; and the geni-*
> *tals, including his perineum.*
>
> *Bring your partner to the brink of orgasm, pull back,*
> *tease again.*
>
> *Unleash the orgasm(s)—manually, orally, and/or via*
> *intercourse.*

What Sex Life Makeover Participants Say

"Blindfold sex is brilliant."

"I had been brainwashed by sex-equals-intimacy doc-
trine. I thought I had to keep my eyes open. Sex was great
this way. It took the pressure off. I am not happy with my
husband's body, but I feel like I should be able to overcome
that. The blindfold took the guilt away."

The Sex Life Makeover Plan

1. Turn yourself on by flirting with a stranger on the train
or at the gas pump across from yours, watching a video
alone, dressing suggestively, and fantasizing erotic encounters before being intimate with your partner. Flirting
is a harmless and healthy activity that makes most of us feel
sexier. Merely exposing a little cleavage can put some
women in the mood.

Most of us fail to nurture our fantasy lives. A steamy fantasy can rev up your erotic engine so that your less-than-
ideal partner seems suddenly more appealing. Eventually

we will all be rather unappealing and dependent on our partners' ability to recall in fantasy our younger, more attractive selves. I suspect that old couples who remain happily in love have the ability to look at each other and see the past. How lucky for them!

❋ Technique Tips ....

THE FANTASY FOREPLAY

Keep a fantasy notebook and jot down erotic ideas or scenarios that excite you. Don't censor yourself. It's okay to fantasize anything. Once you have developed a story line—something as basic as sex on the beach or as complicated as an S-and-M scene set in a European castle— use that fantasy as mental foreplay. Before having sex with your partner, pull out the fantasy.

And develop some fantasies based on memories of your shared erotic past together. Go back to the first time you made love or to a particularly thrilling encounter. Now use those fantasies regularly as mental foreplay.

---

2. Use costumes and role-playing.

Clothes can hide all manner of sins. Every woman knows that. Shop for an erotic wardrobe: silk kimonos and pajamas for both, lingerie that accents her best features, bustiers that cinch the midriff, silk boxers and short robes he can leave on during lovemaking. And masks! Buy feather masks, Mardi Gras masks, satin ones—all manner of masks.

Costumes also make it more possible for you to imagine, even act out, fantasy encounters.

❋ Technique Tips

THE FANTASY ENCOUNTER

Take fantasy out of the realm of personal mental foreplay and use it to excite each other. Share your fantasy notebooks. If you aren't ready to act out a fantasy, talk it through. I cannot emphasize enough the importance of fantasy when there are body issues standing in the way of desire and arousal. You need to get that head involved.

A typical fantasy encounter: He (the less attractive partner) plays voyeur. Pretending to be observing her through his binoculars from a window across an apartment building courtyard, he describes her body in glowing terms. "I see your rosy nipples against your creamy white skin. The curve of your hips is like a sensuous sliver of moon in the sky. . . ." As he describes her body, she touches each part, becoming aroused.

In another fantasy, she (the less attractive partner) plays Cinderella. She describes her perception of him riding past her home in a royal procession. "You stand in the open car, raise your arm to wave, and your biceps are clear beneath your suit jacket. For an instant, you see me hidden behind the curtain. You see only my eyes, but your eyes lock onto mine. I feel my clitoris throb in re-

sponse. . . ." *He comes to her in the dark of night. They make passionate love.*

Use your erotic imagination to create exciting fantasies that make your partner see past the weakness of the flesh to the passion inside.

The Top-ten Fantasy Scenarios

Fantasy is a nearly universal experience, a mental aphrodisiac with amazing powers. Sometimes it is a conscious process, sometimes not. But if you are not satisfied with your sex life and you aren't using fantasy to create and sustain arousal, you are missing something: the fastest and easiest route to getting where you want to be.

People always worry: Are my fantasies "normal"? Does fantasizing mean I want to do something? Is there something wrong with me if I can't come up with a good fantasy?

Unless you have nothing but violent fantasies—and can't become aroused any other way—your fantasies are "normal," whatever that means. Fantasizing does not necessarily mean that you want to do what you are fantasizing. Many people, for example, fantasize homosexual encounters without having the real desire to have a homosexual relationship. And some people have difficulty fantasizing because they censor their erotic thoughts.

Recent studies indicate men and women now have fantasies that are more alike than they were twenty years ago, when sexual fantasies first came under the cultural microscope. According to Nancy Friday, author of Women on Top, among other books about sexual fantasies, women's fantasies have become more graphic and overtly sexual and aggressive. Don't be afraid or ashamed of those fantasies.

Many of us have a "favorite friend" fantasy, that erotic scenario guaranteed to arouse us during masturbation or when arousal subsides during lovemaking. The friend will likely be one of the following types.

THE TOP-TEN SEXUAL FANTASIES

1. Making love with someone other than your regular partner—the most common fantasy for both men and women.

2. The forbidden partner—someone from another race or class, a relative, a friend's spouse.

3. Multiple partners, typically sex with your lover and another person. (For men this "two women" fantasy is a favorite.)

4. The romantic fantasy—sex in idyllic surroundings, such as a beach. (More common for women than men.)

5. Spontaneous stranger encounter—like the "zipless fuck" popularized by author Erica Jong in the classic novel Fear of Flying, in which strangers meet on a train, *for example, and fall upon each other in the nearest sleeping compartment as their clothes simply melt away.*

6. Forced sex—sometimes called "the rape fantasy," and actually common to both men and women. (The fantasy signifies a desire to have sex without guilt or responsibility, not to actually be raped.)

7. "Taboo" sex acts such as having sex in a public place or practicing S/M.

8. Exhibitionist or voyeuristic fantasies in which one is having sex while being watched or watching someone else have sex. (A common version of this fantasy for men is watching a wife or girlfriend make love to someone else.)

9. Homosexual encounter.

10. Sex with a celebrity.

3. Make lighting work for you.

Yes, candles and soft-light bulbs are a cliché—but sometimes a cliché is just what you need.

4. Sign a weight loss/fitness/beauty makeover contract.

Occasionally a man or woman makes outrageous demands on, or has unrealistic physical expectations of, a partner. We've all heard stories about men who want their partners to have breast enhancement surgery, for example, to turn them on again. But the vast majority of people who say their partners no longer arouse them have legitimate gripes. Have you seen those couples makeovers on *Live with Regis and Kelly*? Men and women who haven't been to a dentist or a hairdresser in years—or worn something other than sweat suits—are suddenly transformed in a day.

If you can imagine yourself in makeover "before" shots, it's time for a change. Just starting out on the path to an improved physical image will make you sexier to your lover. Sign on the dotted line.

5. Use intercourse positions that flatter your bodies.

Some women feel self-conscious about being on top because they fear they look fat. And some men feel the same way in the missionary position. A wife who complained that her overweight husband always wanted to be on the bottom because, she thought, he was "too lazy to play the active role in intercourse" was stunned when he told her his true motive for lying flat on his back. "It flattens my stomach out," he said.

When you're on top, wear a shirt or a short robe. She, of course, can also wear a sexy teddy or bustier.

If he is overweight and she is lithe and limber, she can adapt the sitting position to great advantage by leaning backward as he grabs her buttocks and thrusts.

THE REAR ENTRY POSITION

The rear entry position facilitates deep penetration, making it a favorite of couples who are in the mood for hard thrusting. But it has another advantage for these makeover couples: The lack of face-to-face contact makes it easier for either or both partners to fantasize without visual distractions. (He can close his eyes if her ass truly doesn't arouse him.)

In the basic version, the woman is on all fours with the man kneeling behind her. She may lower her upper body so that her chest touches the bed—a variation that makes his penis feel larger by elongating her vagina. Some women experience G-spot orgasms this way.

THE X POSITION

I adapted the X from the Kama Sutra position "Woman acting the part of man." It sounds awkward as you're reading the directions, but it is very comfortable, even for two overweight people. In fact, a couple who hadn't made love in months because of their weight issues tried it and reported: "Great! This worked very well in spite of our tummies. What a revelation!"

Imagine that your bodies form an X with the connection at the genitals. The man sits at the edge of the bed with his back straight and one leg outstretched on the bed, the other outstretched toward the floor, or, if he prefers, braced up on a straight-backed chair placed by

> *the bed. Her back supported by pillows, the woman sits astride her partner, with both legs braced on his shoulders.*
>
> *You won't fall right into this position the first time you do it. But you will the second time around. The genital connection is good. And the weight issue sort of recedes into the background.*

❋ Ravished

She poured some more champagne into her glass and leaned back against the plush sofa cushions. Christina was not much of a drinker. She was feeling the second glass of champagne as the bubbles hit her throat.

Rick smiled at her. It was the slightly smug smile of a man who thought he was in because he got invited upstairs for a drink. Champagne probably sealed the deal as far as he was concerned, but it was the only thing she had cold.

"How old are you?" she asked.

"Twenty-nine."

"Too young."

"I like older women."

He grinned. Too young, she thought, sipping the champagne slowly. She'd left the party with him to make her ex-boyfriend jealous. And how could she not invite him up for a drink after he'd walked her home?

"So how long were you and Todd together?" he asked. He sat

down beside her, put one arm on the sofa behind her, and stroked her arm with his free hand. "Seems like an amicable split."

"Yes," she said.

"You have beautiful skin," he said, caressing her bare shoulder. "Like café au lait."

He was too short and too white. She had never really been attracted to white men. And she didn't like short men at all.

"Thank you," she said, sitting up straighter so he wouldn't get the idea that moving his hand down to her breast was an option.

Then he leaned forward and pulled his sweater off over his head, exposing a very hairy chest. She had forgotten that she did like white-male chest hair. Those long, silky strands felt sensuous between the fingers.

"Oh," she said.

He took the champagne glass out of her hand, set it on the glass-topped coffee table, and kissed her, softly at first, his lips almost softer than a man's should be—then hard, pushing his teeth against hers. She didn't like that kissing style, but it felt good with him.

And his hands seemed to be everywhere as he kissed her. He stroked her back, caressed her neck, fondled her breasts through her silk dress. She closed her eyes and felt one hand move down her body. He squeezed her thigh, then ran his hand along her inner thigh down to the knee and back up so that his thumb rested against the damp crotch of her panties.

"You're hot," he whispered.

He wasn't her type, but her panties were damp already. They made out for a while on the sofa, his hands continuing their exploration of her body unimpeded. She wasn't doing anything except returning his kisses and occasionally pressing her hands into his chest hair. *I should stop this now,* she thought, but she didn't. His thumb was massaging her clitoris through her panties. She was vaguely aware that he was pulling the spaghetti straps off her shoulders one at a time, freeing her breasts and kissing them one at a time.

Breathing heavily, she pulled away from his mouth and said, "We shouldn't. . . ."

"Your nipples are beautiful," he said. "What is that color? Dusty rose?"

He unzipped his pants. His penis was large. What was a penis like that doing on a short white man? She reached for it. He moved closer. She put both hands around his penis, more solid than any piece of flesh she'd ever held in her hands. He was penis-proud. She could see that in his face. Well, who could blame him?

Without letting go of his penis she leaned back into the sofa cushions and opened her thighs. Grasping her hips, he pushed his cock inside her. They fit perfectly, his body not too large, his cock wonderfully so. She felt no emotional interference to throw her off stride as she moved with him. He wedged two fingers between their bodies and held them steady against her clit.

She fucked his hand and his cock. The orgasmic contractions began in short, distinctive little blasts and grew and melded together until her mind was blank. She felt him come inside her in a spray deep and hard, the ejaculation of youth.

When he came, he growled.

Would she ever get used to that?

"More Foreplay, Please!"

Women under thirty-five complain they don't get enough foreplay—although the preferred term among sexperts and therapists is now "loveplay." But here's the surprise: Men over thirty-five have the same complaint: not enough foreplay *from her.* They might not tell their partners they are past the touch-and-go stage but they do report to sex researchers and survey takers that they would like more kissing, hugging, caressing, and fondling. In fact, "more foreplay" is the number one request of the men I've interviewed who are over thirty-five. How did that happen?

As we age, women's physiological responses speed up and men's slow down. She becomes more easily aroused. He doesn't get the automatic erection simply from visual arousal. The problem: She keeps relating to him as if he were twenty-five and quicker to ejaculate than she would like.

The Standard Advice

Spend more time arousing her. Pay particular attention to the kissing and caressing. And—oh, yeah—she should do the same for him too.

That's good advice as far as it goes. You need to take "foreplay" out of the realm of the obvious and mundane. Call it "loveplay" and make it creative and sizzling. Loveplay turns desire into arousal and then into more intense arousal.

And don't be so narrow in your definition. Sex is not just desire, arousal, foreplay, intercourse, release.

> ### The Ultimate Kiss
>
> *Almost a decade ago I interviewed Michel, a charming gigolo, in a romantic Paris bistro. In Europe the life of a gigolo carries less stigma than it does in the United States. Wealthy women loved him and passed him around. Maybe they still do. I like to think so.*
>
> *The secret of pleasing women, he told me, is knowing how to kiss them.*
>
> *"A kiss is sacred. A man enters a woman's soul through kissing her."*
>
> *He kissed my wrist and made a believer of me. In the*

ensuing years I have included the wrist kiss in any number of magazine articles or tips given to interviewers writing articles of their own.

Here is Michel's Ultimate Kiss (which also works on men):

· Kiss the inside of her wrist first. Hold your lips against her wrist until you feel her pulse on your lips. Look into her eyes the whole time.

· Brush your lips across hers lightly. Pull back. Take her face in your hands. Put your lips on hers and press gently as you look into her eyes.

· Close your eyes briefly. Begin kissing her passionately without putting your tongue in her mouth. Open your eyes. Continue kissing her passionately.

· Play with her lips with the tip of your tongue.

· Kiss, lick, and suck each lip in turn.

· Now French-kiss her. Remember to use the tongue lightly. The French kiss is meant to be a passionate yet delicate exploration of the lover's mouth and tongue with your tongue. With the tip of your tongue, play with her tongue, the inside of her lips, the edges of her teeth. Don't thrust your tongue forcefully into her mouth. Lead with the tip. Pull back. Circle your lover's tongue with the tip of yours. Pull back. Lick the sides, undersides, and top of the tongue. Repeat, repeat, repeat. Only when you are both very aroused do you thrust your tongue in and out in rhythmic, stabbing movements.

The Instant First-night Makeover: Erotic Massage

There is no better way for two people to get back in sensual touch with each other than erotic massage. One partner lies naked, facedown, to begin. The other is minimally dressed: she in panties, he in briefs. Sparingly use lotion or oil that you warm in the palm of your hand before applying to your lover's body.

The following directions are written for a woman massaging a man, but obviously can be adapted the other way.

❄Technique Tips

Begin with gliding strokes. Run your hands smoothly in long strokes that blend seamlessly together over large areas of his body. Don't stop to rub, knead, or fondle.

Now make circular motions from the spine, up and to the sides of his body.

Knead gently—not with the vigor a masseuse might use—his shoulders and buttocks. Grasp the flesh into your fingers, then push it out. Don't pummel.

Use single- or two-finger gliding strokes on his inner thighs, the back and sides of his neck, and, if he isn't too ticklish, under his arms.

Have him turn over. Repeat the long, gliding strokes on his chest, stomach, and thighs. Use the single-finger stroke on his face, even the delicate areas like eyelids and

*ears. (I can never resist kissing his face at this point.) Also
run your finger down his throat.*

*Stroke his forehead with the fingers of both hands from
the center to the temples. Press lightly at the temples.*

*Now run your hands in broad, gliding strokes all the
way down his body to his toes.*

HIS GENITALS

*At this point, he probably has an erection. Straddle it
but don't insert it. Lower your breasts to his body and
tease his nipples by rubbing yours across his. Or take your
nipples in hand and rub them across his.*

*In the straddle position, move down his body so that
you end up kneeling between his legs. Take his testicles between your fingers and thumb them gently, one at a time.
Then hold a testicle in the palm of your hand and tickle it
lightly with the pads of your fingers. Now the other one.*

*Hold the base of his penis in one hand and work your
other hand in a circular fashion to the head. Use the palm
of that hand to caress the head of his penis.*

*As if you were building a fire with his penis as the
stick, use a rolling/rubbing motion, starting at the base.
Roll/rub up to the head and back down to the base, keeping his penis between your palms. Start slowly. Increase
speed and pressure as he gets closer to orgasm.*

*Lean forward so that he ejaculates on your breasts. To
make him come quickly, insert a finger in his anus and
press gently.*

HER GENITALS

Stroke her pubic hair (if she hasn't shaved or waxed it off).

Use light circular motions with your fingertips on her genital area. Gently part her labia. Use your fingers to make long strokes on the outside lips. Then curve one or two fingers and use the space between knuckle and joint to massage lightly her inner and outer lips in a back-and-forth motion. Massage her labia and work down to her anus.

Alternate that stroke with one using your thumb or first finger alone.

Rotate your fingers around her clitoris. Stroke down with one finger on either side of her clitoris. Rotate. Stroke down.

If she likes direct clitoral stimulation, you can take it between two fingers and gently rotate. But if, like many women, she can't stand the intensity of that stroke, circle your fingertip above the clitoris (at the twelve-o'clock point).

Add the G-spot stroke: While continuing the twelve-o'clock rotation, insert a finger or two into her vagina, and massage her G-spot. (See directions on page 42.)

Now circle your fingertip rapidly around her clitoris as you're massaging her G-spot. Don't be surprised if she ejaculates with this orgasm.

1. Tease.

Like flirting, teasing is a lost art within the "relation-ship." When men and women are new to each other, they tease naturally. Teasing makes one feel naughty and dan-gerous and definitely in erotic control. The fun should never stop!

Maybe I will and maybe I won't, the tease says, *but if I will, I'll do it when I want. Meanwhile, yearn for me.*

Teasing is an integral part of erotic play, a love game for grown-ups that has two components, the visual and physi-cal tease. Practice both.

✳ Technique Tips

FLAUNT YOUR STUFF

Men want to be voyeurs. We instinctively know that when we're dating them. When we live with them, we for-get. While talking to him (about anything), smooth lotion onto your bare arms or legs. Or lift your hair off your neck as though you're trying to let some of the sultry body heat escape. Or adjust your bra strap.

Old tricks—but they work every damn time.

THE SLOW STRIP

The key is to keep your eyes locked onto your partner while slowly removing your clothes. Wear clothes that can be removed to good visual advantage. No dresses that come off over the head, for example, or tight jeans. Blouses and shirts that can be unbuttoned to reveal sexy lingerie—or a hairy masculine chest—are good. No plain old white underwear for either gender unless plain old white underwear is a turn-on for one of you. And stockings, not panty hose. (Did I mention that I believe panty hose should be declared illegal?)

THE PUBLIC STRIP

No, you aren't taking it all off at the restaurant. Simply declare yourself "hot" and shrug out of a jacket, unbutton some buttons. And maintain eye contact while you do it. In a darkened theater, kick off a shoe, lean toward your partner, and run your foot across the top of his or hers.

PHYSICAL TEASES

Use a calligraphy pen or feather to tease your naked partner, paying particular attention to genitals. Keep an array of sensual objects in the nightstand drawer. I have a collection of feather masks and sometimes wear one while performing fellatio. The feathers dance and tickle in unexpected ways.

Try perfuming only the parts of your body that you want your lover to touch. First, she/he sniffs, then touches.

Lightly flick his hot buttons as you're headed out the

door. Tap his penis through his pants. Cup his buttocks. That bit of chest hair poking out of his collar? Twirl it in one finger. Put both hands flat on his chest, press thumbs to nipples through his shirt. Then go.

Whisper suggestive comments in his ear, touch him in intimate ways, wet your lips and look straight into his eyes—and do these things at times when you can't act upon desire, like out in public or before the kids are put down for the night.

2. Don't stop playing when you start intercourse. Continue caressing, kissing, fondling. Sometimes you may want to stop intercourse and play for a while, then go back to it.

3. Add love bites, pinches, and slaps.

An occasional bite, pinch, slap, squeeze—always done lightly, in the spirit of play—intensifies arousal for some men and women. Slaps are particularly effective on the buttocks because they bring the blood closer to the surface, making this flesh more sensitive to touch. Your partner may enjoy having nipples teased by love bites or pinches. (And some people *hate* it.) Running a fingernail down the skin can also be very arousing (or annoying).

Pay close attention to your partner's reactions.

"We are both forty now, and he needs more foreplay than I do. That was an adjustment. I'm the one ready to pop. He needs stroking."

"Sometimes I want him to take me straight to intercourse after heavy kissing. Most of the time I want him to linger along the way. I see that I hadn't been giving him enough back in the loveplay department. It was all about me."

"My girlfriend is all about the mouth. She wants to kiss and be kissed right up to the climax. Okay, I get it."

Hot Spots

Let's take time out for a basic tutorial on the hot spots, those magic-button places on your bodies. You know where most of them are, but you may not be hitting your partner's—nor he yours—or connecting them to each other's as explosively as you would like. If the hot-spot connection was good, would you be complaining about foreplay?

HERS

THE C-SPOT, *her clitoris: This small pink organ, often compared to the penis because of its shaftlike shape, is located at the point where the inner labia join at the top of the vaginal opening. For the majority of women, the clitoris and the surrounding tissue, or "clitoral hood," is the most sexually sensitive part of the body—the hottest of the hot spots.*

THE G-SPOT: *That small mass of rough tissue about a third of the way up the front vaginal wall may have been named after the German gynecologist Ernst Grafeberg, who rediscovered it in the 1940s, but it was familiar territory to the Indian author of the Kama Sutra five thousand years ago. It swells when stimulated. And, in some women, can produce a tremendous orgasm.*

THE AFE ZONE: *The anterior fornix erotic zone is a small patch of skin closer to the cervix than the G-spot. Stroking the AFE zone makes almost any woman lubricate immediately. (That's how you know you've found it.) A sexologist in Kuala Lumpur rediscovered this area and named it in 1994—but again, the author of the Kama Sutra got there first.*

THE U-SPOT: *We typically don't think of the urethra as a sexy place. But the tiny area of tissue above the opening of the urethra (and right below the clitoris) is a pleasure point. Many women stimulate their U-spots during masturbation without being aware that they are. Men typically discover it by accident while looking for the clitoris. If you've ever thought,* That's not the place, but wait a minute . . . it feels good anyway . . . *he's hit your U-spot with his finger or tongue. And it's a good place for him to shift his attention between orgasms if your clitoris is too sensitive to touch for a few moments.*

Individual hot spots: Some women have very sensitive breasts, particularly the nipples. Other potential hot spots include: inner thighs, behind the knees, hollow of the throat, back of the neck.

HIS

THE H-SPOT: *The head of the penis is his big hot spot. Who doesn't know that? Don't neglect the corona, the thick ridge of skin separating the head from the shaft. It is exquisitely sensitive to touch. Running a finger or tongue repeatedly around it can drive some men wild. This is why the "silken swirl"—swirling the tongue around the corona during fellatio—was a skill practiced by courtesans in centuries past.*

THE F-SPOT: *The frenulum is that loose section of skin on the underside of the penis, where the head meets the shaft. In most men it is highly sensitive to touch. Some men reach orgasm more quickly if you strum the frenulum during fellatio.*

THE R AREA: *The raphe is the visible line along the center of the scrotum, an area of the male anatomy too often overlooked during lovemaking. The skin of the scrotum is very sensitive, similar to a woman's labia. Stimulate the raphe by gently running your fingertips along it.*

THE P ZONE: *The perineum is an area an inch or so in size between the anus and the base of the scrotum—and even more neglected by the average woman than the testicles. Rich in nerve endings, the perineum is the second-*

most-important hot spot for some men. I've included directions for stimulating the P zone throughout the book. It's that important.

THE G-SPOT: *Yes, he has one too, located inside his body behind the perineum. You can reach it in two ways: by pressing the perineum with your thumb or finger, or inserting a finger inside his anus and performing the same come-hither forward stroke that he uses on your G-spot. (Many men love this—and some hate it.)*

INDIVIDUAL HOT SPOTS: *Like women, men have their own individual hot spots, places of great sensitivity. They include ears, neck, inner thighs, temples, eyelids, nipples, and buttocks. When you stroke his body, pay attention to his responses.*

CONNECTING THE SPOTS

You can make sex hotter by hitting the hot spots during oral and manual stimulation and intercourse.

Some suggestions:

During manual foreplay, he can stroke the AFE zone, then the G-spot, and back again. Use clockwise, followed by counterclockwise, strokes.

Don't overlook the U-spot during cunnilingus. Shift from the C-spot to the U-spot when she is close to orgasm. Tease her by going back and forth until she can't take it anymore.

Don't worry about learning how to deep-throat. If you concentrate attention during fellatio on the H-spot,

F-spot, and R area, while not neglecting the P zone, he won't notice or care that you don't take the entire shaft into your mouth.

Make whatever adjustments you need to make in intercourse positions to ensure hot-spot connections between her clitoris, AFE, and G, and his H, F, and R.

In the missionary position, put her feet on his shoulders or pull her knees up to her chest and place her feet flat against his chest. Or have him hold her legs with his forearms under the knees.

In the female-superior position, she should either lean back or forward—more effective at hitting the hot spots than riding straight up.

When using the spoon position, she lies on her side with her back to him, bent slightly at the knees and waist. Also bent slightly at the knees and waist, he enters her from behind. The X position described on page 83 is an excellent position for hot-spot connection—as is the classic Yab-Yum on page 59.

❋ The Buildup

"Come upstairs with me," Nancy Lee said to Charles.

They were sitting side by side on an overstuffed love seat in the dark lobby bar of the Gramercy Park Hotel. She put her hand over his, resting on her stockinged thigh, and ran one finger along his

wrist. His skin was velvety, dark and rich. It felt like a luxury she
shouldn't be able to afford.

"Let's finish our champagne," he said, lifting his glass in salute
to her, pressing his hand briefly and firmly into her thigh.

Suppressing a sigh, she lifted her own glass and tipped it in his
direction. He took a sip of his champagne, set down the glass, and
put his arm around her. His long, supple fingers massaged her neck
and shoulders. "Uhmm," she said. His hands felt surprisingly
strong. She wanted to take off her clothes and see what he could
do with those fingers to the rest of her body.

"Will you photograph me?" she asked. He was a photographer.
They'd met that afternoon at a media event they both were cover-
ing, she as a journalist. "I'd love to have a Charles Weatherly photograph." Actually, she hated to be photographed.

"If you want me to take your photo when we get up to your
room, I will," he said, grinning. "You know I like my white models
naked."

"With heels on. I know. I'm an admirer of your artistic work."

He leaned in closer and brushed her lips with his. She liked the
way he smelled, the mixture of dark skin, a green-scented soap,
and YSL. Liking a man's smell was important to her. She touched
his face. He was the most touchable man she'd been near in a
long time. And she had been touching him, stroking his arm, rubbing his back, making the physical overtures he hadn't been making. Charles's approach to seduction—lie back like a sleek cat and
let her do it—may have been dictated by the fact that they'd met
while he was more obviously working than she was, or by the racial
difference, but she guessed it was more likely his sexual style.

His style was certainly working with her.

"Funny, but I knew you would hate having your photo taken when I met you," he said, his hand caressing her neck. "I knew that right away."

The pitch of his breathing had changed. His eyes were melting into hers. He had the sexiest eyes set in the most serious and proper face, she thought.

"I could swim in your eyes," she told him. "It feels like wading into a muddy creek back home in Alabama—all warm and welcoming and oozing into your body crevices."

He threw back his head and laughed. His bald head gleamed in the dim light. She wanted to see the top of it glittering with sweat between her thighs.

"You have beautiful skin," she said, unbuttoning the top two buttons of his shirt and stroking his fine skin with one finger. He ran two fingers up and down the valley of her cleavage in response. "I love touching you," she whispered.

"Do you intimidate men?" he asked, leaning closer to hear her answer in his ear.

"Do I intimidate you?" she asked.

"Do I look intimidated?" He put his hand back on her thigh, higher up this time, the fingers curved possessively around her flesh. She whispered, "No." He ran one finger inside the lace top. She felt his fingertips burn into her flesh. "Drink your champagne, Miss Nancy Lee," he said.

The soft, erotic pressure of his fingers on her flesh was more intoxicating than the champagne.

"You can call me 'babe,'" she said; and they both laughed and drained their glasses.

In the elevator on the way up to her room, they kissed, eyes open. He held her face in his hands. Outside the door to her room, she took his face in her hands and kissed each eyelid, then ran her tongue down each side of his face from the corner of his eye to his chin. He moaned softly.

The door shut behind them; he pushed her up against it, opened her legs with his thigh, and pressed against her. She groaned. Fingers trembling, she unbuttoned the rest of the buttons on his shirt while he unzipped her skirt. They pulled apart, gazed hungrily at each other, and came back together again in a passionate kiss, all the while yanking at each other's clothes. Naked, they fell to the bed.

Greedily she took in every aspect of his body as he straddled her: the long, elegant penis; the long, slender limbs. He was grace personified. Straddling her chest, he massaged her breasts as she eagerly took him into her mouth. His hands were like plush gloves smoothing the skin in lines radiating out from her nipples. She sucked briefly, then held his penis in her hands. Running her tongue experimentally up and down the shaft of his penis, she inhaled his scent. In one sudden movement, he was down her body and plunging inside her. She felt his body convulse as if he were coming, but he wasn't.

He pulled out of her after a few strokes, lowered his head, and parted her labia with two fingers. As soon as he put his tongue on her clitoris, she was gone. Her first orgasm came in waves around him.

"God, you're something," he said.

She did not know how he could hold back, but he did, shifting from cunnilingus to intercourse to manual stimulation until she'd come over and over again and was weak with the desire to feel him explode inside her. "Please come now," she begged him. He pulled her hips up off the bed, drove into her with fierce passion, and possessed her more completely than any man ever had done.

Part IV

PERFORMANCE

"He Won't Go
Down on Me."

If you are a Boomer, you may think that this complaint belongs to the really older generation. Not necessarily. Though we Boomer women fought for the right to cunnilingus, the generation of women in their twenties now has accepted a sexual status quo even our grandmothers wouldn't tolerate back in the fifties: She expects to perform oral sex but not to receive it. *(We trained our men to give us the first orgasm via cunnilingus—the greatest achievement of the women's movement.)*

Girls go down; boys don't necessarily go down.

The young woman who began performing blow jobs in middle school does often complain in her late twenties after she's settled into a committed relationship that he won't go where she suddenly realizes she'd like him to go. The latest woman to tell me that is a darling twenty-eight-year-old editor who informed me two years ago: "I don't mind that my fiance won't perform cunnilingus. He had a bad experience with a woman doing that once. And he just won't. I don't care. It isn't important to me."

He's her husband now. It's important.

The Standard Advice

Therapists see male avoidance of cunnilingus as an "issue" and advise—of course!—therapy to find out why he is repulsed or frightened by the vagina. (I smell that "bad experience" excuse again.)

Sexperts put his reluctance down to performance anxiety—or perhaps women in his past who didn't smell fresh—and offer convoluted cunnilingus directions. One popular author devotes twenty pages to the "basic" directions.

Women's magazines provide hygiene tips for her. That, of course, includes pubic-hair-management advice. The trend in recent years among women under thirty-five has been toward waxing it all off, with women over thirty-five more often trimming the bush into a discreet shape, something less likely to get caught in the teeth. But some men actually like pubic hair. Work out that hair issue between yourselves.

The big problem with the advice: He doesn't read women's magazines or sex advice books or pay attention to therapist advice on talk shows or online. She has to highlight the directions and hand them to him. Really, there's

no clever and cute way to get the information to him—unless
you want to write it on your inner thighs. Be direct.

What if she's the one who says, "Don't go down on me"?

Often she is the one with the "issues" about cunnilingus. She may not be entirely comfortable with her body or her sexuality. Maybe she hasn't been with a man who knew how to perform cunnilingus well. When a woman tells me, "I don't like it," I know the latter is the case.

If you're that woman, you've been depriving yourself of one of life's greatest pleasures—as well as depriving your man of giving you such pleasure.

The Instant First-night Makeover: Going Down

Tonight's the night you are 1. finally going to do it, or 2. finally going to do it right. And she is finally going to love it.

There are two important things to remember about eating out: Use soft, gentle strokes, paying attention to her cues if she wants more pressure. And don't imitate the exaggerated tongue-flicking that you see porn stars perform. It looks great but isn't that effective.

- Start at the top. Stroke, massage, nibble, suck, kiss, lick, and otherwise tease her body, avoiding the genital area until she is aroused. That's particularly important if she is the squeamish partner!
- Pay special attention to her breasts. Massage her areolae with flat, open palms; then play with the nipples as

you lick and kiss slowly down a line from her navel to the edge of her pubic hair.

- Lick the line of flesh between her pelvis and thighs. Kiss and lick up and down one inner thigh to the area behind her knees. Now the other.
- Get into a comfortable position for both of you. She will be leaning back against pillows either with legs open, bent at the knees, feet flat, or legs outstretched and open in a V. You can lie or kneel between her legs (or come in from the side). She might raise one leg or wrap a leg around your shoulder. And she can sit on your face, actually straddle you and lower her clitoris to your mouth. A lot of women love this position because it puts them in charge.
- Gently part her labia. She may want to use her hand to assist in parting her lips and holding them open, the better for you to lift the clitoral hood. If her clitoris is well back inside the hood, gently run your fingers along the side of the hood to expose the clitoris. (You may need to keep one hand in this position until she reaches orgasm.)
- Lick the delicate tissue along the sides and above and below her clitoris in long, broad strokes of the tongue. Experiment with your tongue strokes.
- Put your lips around the sides of her clitoris. Hold them in a pursed position as you gently suck. Alternate the sucking with licking of the surrounding tissues.
- Some women do not enjoy direct stimulation of the cli-

toris. Others do. If she likes it, you can lick and suck her clitoris.

· When she is nearing orgasm, cover the clitoral area with your mouth. Suck around the sides of her clitoris. Stimulate her labia with your hand or stroke her inner thighs or tease her nipples—or alternate those stimuli. And do not move your mouth until she has reached orgasm, unless you plan to bring her to orgasm via manual stimulation or intercourse.

· Keep in mind that women vary greatly in how much pressure they like, whether or not they want direct or indirect clitoral stimulation, whether they prefer a pattern of repetitive strokes or a lot of variation. She may want you to focus directly on her clitoris only when she is near orgasm. And it is her responsibility to indicate what she wants by moving into you or pulling back, by shifting her body or taking your head in her hands to get you where she wants you to be, by saying, "Yes, yes, yes!" or, "Uhmm . . . over here please."

The Sex Life Makeover Plan

Once a woman has overcome any inhibitions she might have about receiving oral sex and a man has learned how to perform it well, both will likely find this is her surest path to orgasm. A man who "learned how to eat out my woman at age forty using the makeover plan" told me: "A woman is most beautiful when she has surrendered to pleasure. I have seen my wife surrender during intercourse, but this gives me a different and special perspective on that beauty."

This is one of the most rewarding Sex Life Makeovers.

1. Combining manual/oral play.

❋**Technique Tips** ....

> ADD FINGER PLAY
>
> *Insert one or two fingers into her vagina and massage her G-spot as you eat her out. Remember the AFE zone? If she isn't lubricating sufficiently, stroke the AFE. Then go back to the G. Or use your fingers to stroke her perineum or, if she likes it, insert a finger into her anus or simply circle the opening of the anus with a (well-lubricated, of course) finger or two.*
>
> *For many women, the interplay of oral and manual stimulation is incredibly arousing.*

2. Use your face.

Your tongue may get tired before she has reached orgasm. Use your nose and chin to stimulate her clitoris and give your tongue an occasional break.

3. Lick off the honey dust.

Okay, if the taste of female secretions is off-putting to you, buy some honey dust and sprinkle a little on her labia and surrounding area. You can find honey dust in sex-toy stores, some upscale gift boutiques and lingerie shops, and online. It's a fun product, my favorite sex toy. Use occasionally even if you aren't squeamish. (She can dust and lick him too.)

4. Vary the cunnilingus strokes.

Add a few virtuoso tongue moves. I know I told you to eschew that obvious tongue-flick move you see in porn films. (Some sexperts say: Never flick! I don't know how they can be so rigid.) But some women (and I am one of them) enjoy having the tip of his tongue flicked in the right place at the right time.

❄Technique Tips ·······································

THE FLICK

After she has become very aroused, use the tip of your tongue—no broad strokes here—to flick back and forth rapidly along the top of the clitoral shaft. Then flick up and down the shaft. When she is approaching orgasm, flick back and forth across the tip of the clitoris only. Remember: This doesn't work for all women, and it's up to her to let you know if she is one of those who is not aroused/amused by the flick.

THE FLAME

Pretend your tongue is a hot flame. Run that flame up and down her inner thighs, her labia, and finally her clitoris. Keep the flame moving hot and fast around her clitoris. If she wants it to linger long in one place, she will let you know. One man told me: "My lover grabbed my ears and held me there."

THE VELVET NO

Use this technique on multiorgasmic women who want a stronger touch after the first orgasm. Put the tip of your tongue against the shaft of her clitoris and hold it steady. Move your head rapidly back and forth as if you were saying, "no, no, no!" The key to this move is holding that tongue steady.

THE LIP PINCH

Cover your teeth with your lips. Pretend your lips are a set of pincers. Quickly open and shut them around her clitoris (also effective on nipples). The open-and-shut movement must be a series of rapid and extremely gentle repetitions.

5. Suck her breasts.

If she is really slow to warm to cunnilingus, start with her breasts. The mouth movements you make here mirror the ones you will make down below. Women with particularly sensitive breasts love this move—whether they are shy about cunnilingus or not.

> *Kiss her nipples and areolae with light, flitting kisses.
> Follow by gentle nibbling. Run your tongue in circles
> around the areolae and nipples. Make the circles faster
> and faster. Suck her nipple into your mouth, knead it
> gently between your lips, suck again, pull the areola into
> your mouth. Suck in more of her breast, as much as you
> can, and hold it firmly between your tongue and the roof
> of your mouth as you suck.*

What Sex Life Makeover Participants Say

"I thought I didn't like cunnilingus until my boyfriend followed the directions—which he said were simple—and gave
me my first oral orgasm."

"It works best for me if he kisses my clitoris the way he
kisses my mouth—in nice, big, wet, tip-of-the-tongue
kisses. Now he gets that."

"I always wanted to play with her asshole and she
wouldn't let me, but she lets me now because I've learned
how to be so good at cunnilingus she doesn't care what else I
do."

"What kind of lesbian doesn't like cunnilingus?" Mike asked Katie in a teasing voice. She blushed. "Hey, I don't mean to embarrass you!"

Oh, yes, he did. Mike and Katie had been working together for two months and went out together after work like this once a week. He was, she told Michelle, her beer buddy. She didn't add: *And I think about him all the time. I want him to fuck me so bad, I'm crawling the walls of our bedroom every night.*

Katie and Michelle were roommates before they were lovers— and they became lovers because they were both damned tired of men. They had their hearts broken the same weekend and somehow mutual solace turned to something else. Katie liked the relationship part, but she didn't particularly like the sex.

"Well," Mike repeated, "what kind of lesbian doesn't like cunnilingus?"

"I can't believe I told you that," she said. "It's the beer talking."

"You just haven't experienced it done right," he said, with that smug look she recognized from having been told the same thing by other men—who apparently never did it "right" either. She hadn't liked oral sex with them any better than she did with Michelle. "When a man knows what he's doing down there, he can drive you wild, baby, believe me."

They ordered another round and talked about work in a desultory fashion. Then Mike said, "If you ever think about switching teams again, let me know."

She went home that night and, after Michelle fell asleep, e-mailed a friend in another state: *Aaarrgghh . . . what's wrong with*

me? I love Michelle but I want a man. I want to be fucked by a man.
It's all I think about, hard fucking!

Cunnilingus? She didn't think about that at all.

But the next week and the week after that, she went out for beers with Mike on Thursday night and endured his teasing.

"You don't like it with Michelle?" he asked. "What is she doing wrong?"

"Nothing!" Katie declared loyally. *She licks me like an ice-cream cone. Or she licks me like a cat grooming itself.* "She's fine. It's me. I just don't like oral sex."

"Oh, yeah," Mike said, the gleam in his eye, she suddenly realized, much more than the joy of teasing her. His eyes were heavy with desire, like her own. "I bet I could make you like it."

The following Thursday night Michelle was out of town. And what happened next, they acknowledged later, was inevitable. They were only waiting for opportunity to present itself, and on that Thursday night, it did.

He kissed her at the bar, a full-on kiss that made her heart pound, her face sweat, and her chest redden. His mouth was softer than she'd expected it to be, the lips fuller than they appeared, more sensual. As his tongue flirted with hers, she felt shivers in her groin.

"What a kiss." She groaned when they tore themselves apart from each other.

He paid their tab, took her hand, and led her to his apartment down the block. "I shouldn't," she protested in such a soft voice she doubted he heard it over the sounds of the blood thudding in his ears. Inside his apartment, he pulled her awkwardly into his arms.

But the awkwardness disappeared when he began kissing her again. As his tongue explored her mouth, his hands roamed her body, lifting her T-shirt to fondle her breasts, hiking her miniskirt to caress her aching mons. She was so hot for him, she felt dizzy. Somehow they were entangled on his futon without her remembering that they'd walked in that direction—and without him taking his mouth away from hers. Eagerly she helped him tug off her skirt and panties. She was unfastening his belt, desperate to spring his cock free, when he said, "No, not yet."

Not yet?

Suddenly he was between her legs, kissing her labia the way he'd kissed her lips. He put two fingers inside her vagina and stroked her in places she didn't know she had. Writhing beneath his tongue and fingers, she begged, "Fuck me!" He shook his head vigorously no while holding his tongue in place against her clit. She shivered.

His tongue moved in long, slow strokes on the sides of her clitoris, above and below it. He used the tip of it to circle her clitoris until she thought she would go crazy with desire. When was he going to stop and fuck her? His mouth over her clitoris, he gently sucked as he kept up his manual ministrations to her vagina.

The orgasm seemed to start in two places, inside her vagina and in her clitoris. She grabbed the headboard and screamed as the contractions jolted her, spreading like waves throughout her genitals. Crying and panting, she came over and over again beneath his tongue.

When at last he came up, his face glistened with her juices. He fucked her. And it was the most amazing fuck of her life.

"She Rarely Performs Fellatio."

Probably the number one sexual complaint I've heard from men about their wives and girlfriends is: "She stopped giving head when we got married (or started living together or were together for a year)." Women acknowledge that they expect to perform fellatio when they're dating but "not so much" when they're in a relationship. And surprisingly, most women think this is okay.

It is definitely not "okay" with their men. He might *want* anal sex but he feels *entitled* to oral sex. As long as he's clean and doesn't force himself upon her in a rough and unwelcome manner, he *is* entitled.

In the twenty-first century, any sophisticated man or woman who would deny a lover the pleasures of the tongue should not be surprised to receive their walking papers.

The Standard Advice

Therapists advise therapy for her "issues." Sexperts offer frenzied fellatio instructions. Women's magazines throw in hygiene tips for him.

The problem with the therapists' advice: If she had any real "issues" with fellatio, she wouldn't have performed it on him while they were dating. And the problem with the sexperts' advice: These days they make every sexual act too complicated—more to top themselves (in the previous book) and the competition, thus assuring the next book contract, rather than serving readers' real needs. How likely is it that a woman who isn't doing the basic blow job will work her way through a dozen or more pages of virtuoso directions tonight?

The Instant First-night Makeover: A Basic Blow Job

The two most important things to remember when performing a blow job:

- No head bobbing. It just looks silly. Move his penis, not your head.
- And keep your tongue moving all the time.

This is the basic black dress of blow jobs. You can never go wrong with it. And variations (ways of accessorizing) are a few pages over as well as scattered through other makeovers.

- *Kiss and lick his inner thighs while pulling down ever so gently on his scrotum. With your finger pads, scratch his testicles. Put his balls carefully in your mouth one at a time. Roll them around. Then, again ever so gently, pull them down with your mouth.*

- *While you are attending to his balls, run your fingers lovingly up and down the shaft of his—I'm betting— erect penis.*

- *Get into a comfortable position, either kneeling at his side on the bed at a right angle to his body or kneeling between his legs. Or you can bring him down to the edge of the bed and kneel on the floor. Wet your lips and be sure that your lips cover your teeth. (No accidental biting.) Run your tongue around the head of his penis to moisten it.*

- *Hold the base of his penis firmly in one hand. (With the other hand, you can form a circle of your thumb and first finger—what sexpert Lou Paget calls "the ring and the seal" to elongate your mouth and prevent him from going in farther than you would like. Use that hand in a twisting motion as you fellate him.) Or if his erection is not firm, you can use both hands in the twisting upward stroke (page 15).*

- *Circle the head with your tongue in a swirling motion, then work your tongue in long strokes up and down his shaft. Now back to the head.*

- *Follow the ridge of the corona with your tongue while working the shaft with your hands, the penis sandwiched in between them (unless, of course, you want to keep that "ring and seal" in place the whole time—your call).*
- *Pay attention to the frenulum and the raphe.*
- *Make eye contact with him from time to time if you can.*
- *Do at least ten or twenty seconds of the showy move (like the ice skater's triple jump): Repeatedly move his penis in and out of your mouth as deeply as you want to go—while keeping that tongue in motion.*
- *Go back to the head. Now apply gentle pressure with thumb or finger pads to his perineum. Swallow. (Details on page 60.)*

  He loves you. He really loves you.

The Sex Life Makeover Plan

It's fellatio week at your house. And you have no idea how loving, generous, and kind a man can be when he's this satisfied.

1. Substitute the breast.

Men love breast play. This little move is something he's likely fantasized, if not experienced. Take his erection firmly in hand and glide it between your breasts. Now

squeeze them together as he thrusts between them. De-
pending on the size of his penis, the size of your breasts,
your position and his, you might be able to lick or suck the
head on the forward thrust. This doesn't replace fellatio on
a regular basis, but it can be an occasional substitute when
you're just not in the mood to perform.

2. Role-play.

Acting out a simple fantasy scenario doesn't require real
acting skills. Why pretend? It's exciting. And much of your
arousal and his grows out of the act. Your technical performance skills won't be tested here, making this another
game for those nights when you're not exactly in the mood
but don't want to refuse him.

Allow him to "force" you to "suck his cock." He stands
with legs spread. You kneel before him. Be sure to use the
"ring and seal" because he will be thrusting more vigorously
than normal. And hold on to the base of his penis. Not a lot
is required of you beyond a fast-moving tongue and getting
your head into an optimum position for receiving his ejaculate without choking.

This is a thrilling bit of theater to act out in a semipublic
place, like, for example, a dark corner in a dark club.

3. Quid pro quo: the "69" position.

This is not a favorite of mine because I like to commit
myself fully to either giving or receiving oral sex. But it is a
nice diversion from time to time. And it looks sexy.

Either partner can be on top, or they can lie side by side as he performs cunnilingus and she fellatio. You may actually get more control if you're flat on your back and he is straddling you. Because a skilled performance requires concentration, neither partner will be as adept as they are working alone. But the intimacy achieved is rewarding.

Try alternating actively stimulating each other. When he is active, she can hold his penis in her mouth or even outside her mouth, where it will be stimulated by her hot breath. When she is actively stimulating him, he can rest his mouth on her vulva so his hot breaths rather than his tongue tickle her.

4. Add variations to the basic blow job.

Relax. I'm not giving you twenty pages of diagrammed moves. These are a few ways of adapting the basic technique. There are more in other sections of this book. You will discover others on your own. Don't forget that every man is different, and what works for one won't necessarily work for the other.

THE DEEP SUCK

Gradually suck into your mouth as much of the shaft of his penis as you can and still continue the sucking motion. Your tongue against the roof of your mouth creates most of the suction. But you can also pull in the sides of your cheeks to create suction. Open your mouth to release it. Try to relax the back of your throat so you don't trigger a gag reflex. If you are straddling him facing his feet, your throat and mouth will be a good angle for the deep suck—even for pulling off the showy "deep throat" if you like.

STRUMMING

Flick your tongue lightly and rapidly back and forth across the delicate corona. After several flicks, run your tongue from base to head, then flick it up and down the same path before resuming your ministrations to the corona.

Use the same move on the frenulum.

THE FULL TONGUE

Most fellatio moves involve the tip of your tongue. Try using the top, sides—the full tongue. The same move with more tongue will feel new and different to him.

What Sex Life Makeover Participants Say

"Fellatio is the deal breaker. It's not a sex life without oral sex."

"I didn't like giving head because I was never completely convinced I knew what I was doing. The pages of directions in some books did put me off. This really works for me—and my guy seems happier."

✳ Her Turn

Jasmine never had to try hard. Blond hair, big blue eyes, ivory complexion, long legs, and lovely breasts—she was the woman most men fantasize taking to bed. And when a man won that coveted prize, her sexual acquiescence, she arranged herself artfully in erotic poses and let her beauty inspire him to whatever sexual heights he could reach.

Men, she sometimes complained to girlfriends, weren't that good in bed. She had a vibrator in a shade of pink that almost matched her inner lips. "I love my vibrator," she told the same friends. "Men are nice for the cuddle and kiss, but they don't get you off."

And then she met Alex.

She had her first oral orgasm with him. Lying on top of his bed covered in a cheap fabric meant to represent silk, she writhed and twisted, grasping slippery handfuls of the fabric, the same stuff that slid under her heels. The sensations were so intense that she lost all control and felt like she was going down a waterslide into paradise.

"Oh, my God!" She gasped when it was over. "That was the best sex I ever had."

"Yeah?" Alex said, his face wet with her, a look of frank puzzlement in his eyes.

Oh, she couldn't wait to tell her girlfriends that she'd found an amazing lover, and he didn't even know how good he was!

Over the next several days Alex had her in every way possible. His wickedly talented fingers found a place inside her that made her juices run with one or two strokes. He licked her clitoris and probed her G-spot and made her explode into an ecstasy that wrapped itself around his hands and his mouth, and suffused her whole body. They had intercourse in every position she'd ever imagined and then some. He left her breathless and gasping, sore and tired, and yet wanting more and more.

Sometimes he guided her head to his penis. She licked dutifully. When he groaned and pulled away after a few licks, she realized that he just couldn't take much stimulation there and was reluctant to try again.

Alex was so good in bed that she let the little pink vibrator rest in its case.

Happy didn't begin to describe her state of mind, until he said, "Jasmine, this isn't working out for me."

"What?" she said, suddenly light-headed and afraid she might faint. "What isn't working out for you? Alex, you're a wonderful lover. I am happy with you."

"I know," he said. "And I'm sorry to let you down. I thought about taking the easy way out, not calling, but I'm just not that kind of guy."

"Alex!" she wailed. Tears spilled out of her eyes. "I don't understand! Are you afraid of love and commitment? Is that it?"

She looked at him hard. Alex was twenty pounds overweight, barrel-chested, already losing his hair at thirty-two. And he wasn't rich. He didn't take her to the kind of places other men did. No gifts, unless you counted the supermarket bouquets.

"You can't do this to me," she said in quiet fury. "Who do you think you are?"

He got what she was saying and shot her a look of pure rage.

"Jasmine, you're a lousy lay. A beautiful girl, but a lousy lay." As he walked out the door, he added: "You don't know how to give head, Jasmine. It's a basic requirement in a civilized sexual exchange between the male and the female. Get a book and a banana. It's not that hard to learn.

"Good-bye, Jasmine."

Alone in her lovely bedroom, stretched out gracefully across the real silk spread in a flattering shade of blue, she sobbed. *How dare he—how fucking dare he?* When she was able to speak and called her girlfriends, she was beyond shocked when they said, Yes, a book and a banana . . . not a bad idea at all.

Green bananas, she discovered, worked best. As she plied her tongue up and down the shaft of the banana, book in one hand, she imagined that it was Alex's thick cock she held. Perfecting that little swirling movement around the end of the banana, she pictured his huge, glistening penis going into her mouth. She heard him moaning and felt him clutching her head as his penis broke into throbbing spasms, shooting hot, sweet come down her throat.

When she'd had her way with several dozen bananas, she left their limp bodies in the trash can, dressed to thrill in short, sexy black and high-heeled strappy sandals, and took a cab to the hotel where Alex tended bar.

"Jasmine," he said smoothly as he poured her a glass of white wine. "On the house."

She'd been there an hour when she had her chance. The bar was empty except for her. She signaled for Alex, took his hand, and inserted one of his fingers into her mouth. His eyes widened as she treated that finger like a miniature penis and gave it "head."

He asked the hostess to watch the bar for him, guided Jasmine to the elevator, and pushed the button for the nineteenth floor. She put her hand on the bulge inside his pants and squeezed. When they got off the elevator, he led her to a storage closet. Inside, he 129

Performance
unzipped his pants while she sank to her knees.

She grasped the base of his penis firmly in one hand and applied her mouth to him, doing all the tricks she'd learned in that book. He grasped her head just as she'd known he would while she was strumming his frenulum, flicking her tongue back and forth across that piece of tender skin, driving him crazy. When she knew he was ready to come, she leaned her head back at an angle and pressed that tiny indentation in the space between his anus and the base of his balls.

He did shoot the hot, sweet come down her throat.

When they were back in the elevator, both wiping perspiration from their brows, he said, "I'll call you."

"Sure," she said—and had her phone numbers changed the next day.

But she was always grateful to Alex. She might never have landed that extremely rich husband without his help.

"He Loses His Erection During Lovemaking."

Everyone takes erectile failure personally. He feels less a man. She feels less a woman. (*I'm not exciting enough for him. . . . I'm not doing it right. . . . He's cheating on me with his assistant.*) Most of us behave as though the penis were a car that had died in traffic with a big SUV coming up fast in the rearview mirror.

Really, it's not all that. Lost erections are nearly always found again—if not tonight, then the night after. And tonight you can still have a lot of fun with whatever he's got left.

The Standard Advice

Therapists say the obvious: Physical causes should be ruled out. Then assume it's an intimacy issue.

Sexperts say: Perform fellatio. Ignore his erection loss and ask him to pleasure you. Reassure him that it happens to every man and doesn't matter.

Physical causes *can* be the problem. If he is overweight, on medication, has been drinking heavily or overeating, erection loss during lovemaking is likely more than an occasional event. But it does happen to every man at least now and then. No point saying his flaccid penis doesn't matter when it does. That's like him saying, "Of course you don't look fat in that dress," when you clearly do.

Deal with it. Try not to make him feel any worse—but deal with it. If you both can ignore his erection and let him pleasure you, that's a good solution. But it's not the only one.

The Instant First-night Makeover:
The Perfect Stand-up Kiss

Fellatio as you typically perform it may not be enough to wake him up tonight. This one is almost guaranteed to do it—even if he thinks he's lost the will to go on. (The caveat: If he's drunk, there's nothing you can do to counteract those drinks hanging on the end of his penis.) The secret: Combine mouth and firm hand moves and don't overlook his testicles and especially his perineum, that smooth patch of skin between his anus and the base of his testicles where rich nerve endings abound.

Hold his penis firmly in one hand. Take it into your mouth, moving the top third of the shaft in and out. Use the fingers of your other hand to stroke his perineum in a light, tickling come-here fashion.

When he becomes erect, use one hand to do the circular twisting motion described on page 15 at the same time you swirl your tongue around the corona (the ridge separating the shaft from the head of his penis). Pay particular attention to the frenulum (the small piece of skin where the head meets the shaft). Alternate the swirl with the butterfly flick: flicking your tongue back and forth across the corona.

Continue the hand move while taking his testicles in your mouth, one at a time, and sucking lightly. Flick your tongue rapidly across his perineum. Go back to his penis and alternate swirling, flicking, and sucking. Remember: Don't take his penis too far into your mouth when you suck or you won't be able to pull off the suction.

The Sex Life Makeover Plan

1. Buy him a cock ring.

At a sex-toy shop or online store, choose a latex or leather cock ring, a sex toy that sustains erection by restricting blood flow out of the penis. Place it around the base of his penis and scrotum. The resulting pressure is pleasurable for him, heightening sensation in the penis and testicles. Some men report that their erections are harder when they wear the rings.

But he shouldn't wear a ring longer than thirty minutes at a time. Leave it on too long and he may experience pain or bruising.

2. Combine a hand trick with the female-superior position to create an instant, usable erection. No matter what position he was in when he lost the erection, get on top now that it's gone.

✳ Technique Tips

Straddle him. Grasp the base of his penis firmly in one hand—as if you were going to give him a hand job. Use the head of his penis to stroke and stimulate your genitals. When you are ready, lower your body onto his penis (without letting go of the base). Good PC muscles are important here. If you have them, you can grasp the first third of his penis, using your own muscles to simulate thrusting. (That alone may revive his erection.)

Should he remain flaccid, lean forward, supporting yourself on one hand resting beside his body, and work his penis up and down—also using your PC muscles at the same time—to bring yourself to orgasm. Alternate thrusting with the head stroke: using the head of his penis to stimulate your clitoris.

Whether he comes along for the ride or not, this will take you where you want to go.

3. Talk him up—and use your most seductive voice. Language can be as effective as hand tricks. Some men get erect again if they're verbally abused, others if they hear their fantasies described in lavish detail. Does he ask you to talk dirty to him? Does he like phone sex?

If the answers are yes, he can be talked up. Some women feel guilty or embarrassed about dirty talk. Consider your voice—and the words you say—another arousal tool, just as your lips, tongue, hands, and body are.

❊ Technique Tips

Learn the words. Erotic novels are filled with euphemisms for genitals and their interactions. Cocks thrust and plunge. Pussies are juicy. It's a hot, wet, sensual universe below the belt.

Blindfold yourself and listen to an erotic video or DVD. Make note of the dialogue in both X-rated and mainstream R-rated films. Closer, starring Julia Roberts, is perhaps the most verbally erotic film ever made.

If talking dirty is still difficult for you, pretend that you are an actress playing a part.

4. Remember the perineum. Some men regain their erections almost instantly when their perineums are massaged. Use your finger pads or fingernails to stroke or lightly tickle. Press your thumb lightly into his perineum. Release. Press lightly again. Two to four presses should do it.

5. Try "Heat and Ice." The late renowned erotic writer Marco Vassi once told me in the space of a commercial break on a talk radio show where we were improbably booked together that "running hot and cold" was a "mild form of kinky sex." Marco—who was beyond kinky and was on intimate terms with every bodily secretion—and I—whom he laughingly called the PTA Mom of Sex—had almost no common ground except that he inspired me to try Heat and Ice, a technique I immediately knew belonged in my tricks bag.

Marco's novels are largely out of print, but you should look for them anyway. They are awesome in their erotic power.

✱Technique Tips

While performing oral sex, vary the temperature of your mouth. Start with normal body temperature. Then, using your hand to stimulate your partner, fill your mouth with ice cubes. Wait until your tongue is numb before spitting out the ice. Apply your frozen assets to his genitals. This will feel like a jolt of sexual electricity to him.

After a few minutes, when your oral temperature is back to normal, repeat the procedure, this time filling your mouth with a hot drink.

This method of alternating temperatures restores erection in most men and can prolong the arousal phase for some men. Others say they have more intense orgasms when heat and ice are applied.

"Sometimes the best thing to do with a lost erection is not try to find it. I am over forty and overweight, at the point in my life where I would rather pull out all the stops in pleasing her than try to get it up again."

But from a younger and fitter man: "The techniques really do help. I work long hours, and the erections do fizzle out some nights. I want to get them back. I feel frustrated the next day if I didn't come."

And from his wife: "The stand-up kiss is awesome. I feel like a goddess."

✖ Raising Jonathan

She met Jonathan in an artfully grungy little bar in Austin, Texas, the kind of place where people who played in bar bands went on nights they didn't have gigs. He was dressed like a cowboy, a pretty good indication that he wasn't, and he looked like he would get drunk fairly quickly if something didn't stop him. In other words, he was as much a hard drinker as the bar was a tough watering hole. Carrie thought he could pass for Brad Pitt's stand-in on a movie set, more than good enough for tonight. She had an undifferentiated ache in her private zone, and she needed to put something in there fast. He grinned shyly at her. She let him know she was checking him out, and he self-consciously thrust his pelvis forward, projecting a sizable bulge beneath the soft, worn jeans.

He had a big cock. She knew she could have him if she wanted him, right there in the bar, back in one of the unisex johns where the nicest people sometimes did it drunk. Afterward he would be grateful and apologetic because he would think he'd seduced her and, if she read him right, already half in love.

"Wanna dance?" he asked. "You do the Texas two-step?"

"Sure," she said. "Do you?"

It turned out he was from Chicago and didn't know the two-step from the shuffle and grind that he'd likely been doing on dance floors since his senior prom. He held her in a shoulder hug, his hot breath on her neck sending shivers up and down her spine, and insinuated his body against hers very gently, giving her the opportunity to pull away. She felt that penis, strong, insistent—and, yes, big. And she did not pull away.

"How's Steve?" someone called out to her from across the room.

She raised her eyebrows in a noncommittal way. Steve left her a month ago, and just about everybody knew that, including the weasel who'd called out.

"Steve the boyfriend?" Jonathan asked, a wary look in his eye. "Is this about making him jealous?"

"Husband. Soon to be ex."

"Divorce is tough," Jonathan said, his big brown eyes expressing sympathy for her. "I'm sorry," he whispered into her hair. His hand on her back was strong but gentle. She liked the way he touched her.

When the music stopped, she led him straight out the door and to her car. Glancing back at him, she thought he looked dazed and confused. But he followed her.

"I'm taking you home for the night," she said. "We'll leave your car here and take mine."

"Do you want to go somewhere for dinner first?" he asked.

"I'll make a snack," she said.

In the car she took his face in her hands and kissed him hard on the mouth. His lips, soft yet firm, parted and he covered her hands with his, loosening their pressure on his face as he did. The tip of his tongue expertly licked her lips, inside and out, and flirted with the tip of her own. She sighed. Gaining confidence, he slid one hand between her damp thighs.

As his fingers worked their way inside her panties, he asked, "He's not living there, right?"

"Who?"

"Steve. Your husband."

"Oh, no, don't worry about it. He doesn't live there anymore."

By the time she drove to her house, a mile outside Austin, he had clearly developed performance anxiety. His hand between her legs felt frozen with tension, and the bulge in his jeans was noticeably softer. *Oh, nice,* she thought. She knew she'd come on too strong with him, but she wanted that cock. She squeezed her thighs together around his hand.

"Hey, baby," she said gently. "We're here."

His hand reflexively curled, his fingertips pressing lightly into the flesh of her inner thigh. He looked scared at first, but quickly covered it up with a jaunty "Hey, baby," of his own. *Okay,* she thought, *get him inside and get him up again.*

As he unbuttoned his shirt in the bedroom, she noticed that his fingers trembled slightly, but he'd regained his erection. He grinned at her and pulled her into his arms. She buried her face in his chest, taking a clump of hair into her teeth and pulling gently.

"Nice," he said. "You're a creative kind of gal. I could tell that right away."

He pulled her breasts out of the tight V-neck T-shirt and ran his tongue in circles around each nipple. With one hand he stroked her back while the other worked its way into the jeans she was struggling to discard. He rubbed her clit with his thumb. That only intensified her need to get him inside her as fast as she could.

She slid down his body, unzipped his jeans, and took his cock into her hand. Holding the base firmly, she put the head into her mouth and sucked. He tasted of sweat, but she didn't care. She craved that cock so much that she felt her vagina contract in anticipation as she sucked him. He put his hands on her head. Her tongue swirled around the head, up and down the shaft, back to the head, furiously licking. Then she went back to sucking. She felt him throb inside her mouth. Before he exploded there, she guided him down to the floor on top of her.

"Fuck me," she begged. And she was whimpering by the time he rammed his full length inside her. "Harder." She gasped. He pulled almost out and shoved hard back into her repeatedly, giving her exactly what she wanted. She came convulsively after a dozen strokes—and came again and again.

When he was spent, he curled up around her body, rested his head on her breast, and moaned softly. He told her how wonderful she was. She stroked his face and whispered words of praise into his ear. Under those tender ministrations, he fell softly asleep. She slid out from under him, grabbed a pillow off the bed for his head, tossed an afghan over him, and let him sleep. A few hours later she woke him again with her mouth. When he tried to return the oral favor, she wouldn't let him. She wanted nothing but that big gorgeous cock inside her.

In the morning she drove him back to Austin and dropped him off in the bar parking lot beside his car.

"I want to see you again," he said.

"I'll call you," she said, but she didn't look in the rearview mirror as she pulled away.

✳ *ten*

"She/He Won't Try Anything New in Bed."

I have learned through countless interviews over the years that the phrase *won't try anything new* is inevitably code for: *We have sex in the same limited, uninspired way every time we do it.*

This is a deep sexual performance rut. And couples who are stuck in this rut usually can't work themselves out of it simply by switching their steps or adding a new twist to their signature sex moves. (See chapter one.) They don't have that many steps to switch or moves to adapt. These men and women are lacking an erotic imagination. They didn't get to this place because they had a lot of good ideas or even a few of them. Typically one isn't pushing for anal sex or spanking while the other holds out. It's a lot worse than that. Maybe they don't even have oral sex. One or both are likely sexually inhibited, perhaps with ingrained

....

theories about what is "right" and "wrong" behavior even between consenting married adults in their own bed.

When sexual performance is limited and strictly routine, couples find themselves having sex less and less often. They may eventually become "no sex" couples. It is estimated that approximately 20 million married couples (from all age groups) fall into that category.

The Standard Advice

Therapists say: Talk about the problem and come up with new ways to make love. It's worth noting here something that applies throughout this book: The average therapist or therapist/author bases all their conclusions on a small sampling, their practice or the rare university-funded research study. They do not interview people who don't go into treatment or couples who have garden-variety sex issues or problems—and that is most people. Even the typical research study that winds up being highly touted in the media involves fewer than fifty people—often far fewer. The next headline that supposedly defines your sexual behavior could be taken from the results of a study based on twelve graduate students in Dr. Expert's control group.

Sexperts say: Learn new sex techniques and surprise him/her with your moves tonight.

This advice is more wrongheaded than expert sex advice typically is because it overlooks the obvious: Rut dwellers are not good sexual communicators and—for reasons of shyness, inhibition, lack of creativity—they aren't likely to

initiate surprises for each other either. They need a game
plan more than most couples do.

The Instant First-night Makeover: Learn How to Breathe

Start with a completely nonthreatening activity that will nevertheless energize both of you sexually: Tantric breathing.

✳ **Technique Tips** ....

THE BREATH OF FIRE

Use this before or during lovemaking to get you into the mood or increase arousal, especially if you have trouble getting aroused and/or achieving orgasm. There's no simpler way to oxygenate the blood, a process that increases sexual energy and elevates desire. Take rapid, rhythmic, and shallow breaths through the nose. Keep your mouth closed. Breathe this way for one to three minutes every day if possible—and, of course, during sex.

In this step of your makeover, do the breath of fire together for three to five minutes. Then add:

FIRE BREATHING

Similar name, different technique. Practice it alone (side by side) before incorporating it into lovemaking.

Lie on your back, knees bent, feet spaced well apart. Start by taking deep breaths: Pull each breath into your body so deeply that you feel your diaphragm expanding. Imagine this huge intake of air going all the way down into your genitals. When you exhale, push that air all the way out through your genitals and out of your body.

After a dozen or so deep breaths, pant *by breathing rapidly from your belly with your mouth open. Do this ten or twenty times, then* breathe deeply, *inhaling through the nose and exhaling through the mouth. Make the breathing a continuous circular motion. Imagine a circle of fire, beginning as a small circle composed at first only of nose and mouth, then expanding to include chest, belly, and finally genitals. Feel the erotic heat moving in a circle throughout your body as you breathe.*

And feel your arousal growing with every breath.

Now turn to each other and make love, slowly and sensually, maintaining your breathing techniques as much as possible. Concentrate on arousing each other. Don't worry if lovemaking results in orgasms tonight or not. Your goals are: Learn the breathing skills and get aroused.

The Sex Life Makeover Plan

1. Learn the new basics—the intercourse positions.

Your basics now are the equivalent of a wardrobe that would fit into a tote bag. I want you to expand that selection to the point where you would need at least a roller bag to accommodate the various pieces. To begin, take one night to

see how your bodies fit together in each of the six basic intercourse positions.

No pressure to perform.

✳ Technique Tips

THE FEMALE-SUPERIOR (OR WOMAN ON TOP) POSITION

This is generally considered the most favorable posi-
tion for female orgasm because she has the freedom to
stroke her clitoris during intercourse—and to control the
depth and angle of penetration and the speed of thrust-
ing. He can also fondle her genitals or breasts. And it pro-
vides him with visual stimulation.

In the basic version of the position, she squats or sits
astride the man, who is lying on his back. Her legs are
bent at the knees, one on either side of his body. She may
lean forward or backward, using her hands for support,
or sit upright, keeping both hands free.

THE MISSIONARY (OR MAN ON TOP) POSITION

Legend has it that Pacific Islanders named the posi-
tion after the missionaries who had sex only this way.
The position has been unfairly maligned ever since. It's a
great position for hard thrusting and emotional contact.
Many women as well as men love it.

In the basic version of the position, she lies on her back
with her legs slightly parted. He lies on top of her, support-
ing his weight at least partially with his hands or elbows.
They can lessen or increase the depth of penetration

by putting pillows under the small of her back or wrapping her legs around his waist or placing her feet on his shoulders.

REAR-ENTRY POSITION

Women love this or they don't. Men generally do. The position facilitates deeper penetration than the other basic positions.

In the basic version of the position, she is on all fours with him kneeling behind her. She can change the angle of penetration by lowering her chest to the bed. That also leaves a hand free for stimulating her own clitoris.

SIDE-BY-SIDE (OR SPOONS) POSITION

In the basic version of the position, he faces her back. Her buttocks are angled against him as he puts one leg between hers. Or she can lie half on her back, half on her side, drawing up the leg upon which she is lying. He faces her.

Penetration is limited in the spoon position—which is undoubtedly why the French call it la paresseuse, *meaning "the lazy way."*

SITTING POSITION

He sits in a chair or on the bed with her astride him. Again, penetration is shallow. But they can make it a more vigorous position if he grasps her buttocks and she leans back while he thrusts.

STANDING POSITION

Having intercourse while standing satisfies a need some of us occasionally have for dramatic, urgent lovemaking. It's a great way to begin making love. You can always slide to the floor and finish in another position.

In the basic version of this position, he squats slightly while she lowers herself onto him. She wraps one leg around his waist and he holds her buttocks.

2. Learn the new basics—oral skills.

Take turns performing oral sex on each other. See the directions for fellatio on page 121 and cunnilingus on page 113.

Go for orgasms tonight. It doesn't matter if you climax orally or move from oral sex to intercourse.

3. Learn the new basics—manual skills.

Now take turns manually stimulating each other. See the directions for stimulating him on pages 90–91 and her on page 92.

Again, have orgasms via manual or oral stimulation or intercourse.

4. Go to a bookstore (online is fine too) and buy a selection of sex guides and magazines containing sex advice articles. Each pick a new move to do together at home. Now that you know the basics, you can adapt any position or

technique and incorporate it into your lovemaking reper-toire. And, yes—orgasms!

What Sex Life Makeover Participants Say

From a thirty-four-year-old woman married ten years: "We had almost stopped having sex. Before the makeover, here was our pattern: Deep kissing, he played with my breasts, I grabbed his penis and squeezed it a few times, we got into position and had intercourse."

And her husband adds: "We were very inhibited people without entirely realizing that we were. I'd read sex articles in magazines occasionally, and I am sure she had too. But I could never apply the advice until we had a plan to follow."

The Orgasm Primer

Again, this is information everybody can use. But it is very likely that the couple in this rut knows less about orgasms than the average couple does. Both he and she are probably conditioned to reach orgasm in exactly the same way every time. She may not be orgasmic in most of her encounters. Sometimes couples in this category report that she is not orgasmic during lovemaking at all.

HER ORGASM

When a woman is aroused, blood flow increases to the vagina, swelling the inner and outer labia and the clitoris and causing lubrication. With enough intense physical and psychological stimulation, she will reach orgasm, during which the vagina, sphincter, and uterus contract simultaneously and the blood congested in the vaginal area suddenly rushes back to the rest of the body.

The entire set of contractions generally lasts three to twenty seconds, with intervals of less than a second between the first three to six contractions. Some women experience single orgasms lasting a minute or more, or feel postorgasmic (milder) contractions for up to a minute, or experience an orgasm that seems to radiate throughout their bodies.

Her orgasms may originate from stimulation to:

- THE CLITORIS. *At least two-thirds of all women need clitoral stimulation to reach orgasm. It obviously follows that unless most women adapt the basic intercourse positions and/or use additional manual stimulation, they won't reach orgasm via intercourse alone.*

- THE G-SPOT. *See page 42. Women who have G-spot orgasms report that they feel "deeper" than clitoral orgasms.*

- THE VAGINA/CERVIX. *Some women do reach orgasm via vigorous thrusting during intercourse.*

- THE ANUS. *Anal stimulation also triggers orgasm in some women, possibly because it stimulates the G-spot from a different angle.*

And often a woman who responds to multiple stimuli has a blended orgasm—*the result of stimulation to two or more of her trigger zones. These are the most intense orgasms you'll ever have.*

HIS ORGASM

Most sex therapists, sexologists, and researchers say that male orgasm and ejaculation are the same thing. There are some, however, who claim that men can learn to reach orgasm without ejaculating. (See page 198 for directions.) The pleasurable sensations of male orgasm—the question of ejaculation aside—are rhythmic contractions like the female orgasm but typically lasting from two to ten seconds, a shorter time frame than hers. Upon orgasm, the engorged blood vessels that have been sustaining erection send that blood back into the body, resulting in a flaccid penis.

Men typically reach orgasm (and ejaculate) from stimulation to the penis during intercourse, or oral or manual play. Some men also reach orgasm if their perineums or anuses are massaged, triggering the male G-spot orgasm. (See page 35.) While women can easily learn how to have multiple orgasms, few men can.

Generally speaking, the male orgasmic response is more certain than the female, but less diffuse, and its potential for expansion more limited.

EXTRAGENITAL ORGASMS

Some women—and almost no men—can reach orgasm without genital stimulation. When it does occur, extragenital orgasm usually follows orgasms that were triggered by stimulation to the genitals. A highly orgasmic woman, for example, can reach the third, fourth, fifth, or more orgasm by having her breasts or nipples stroked and massaged. (At that point, some of us can do it by squeezing our thighs together in rhythmic fashion.) It's not so much a talent or learned skill as a blessing.

A rare man may be so blessed.

Some years ago I attended a workshop in "spontaneous orgasm" led by the multitalented performance artist/writer/sexologist Annie Sprinkle. Through using a combination of fire breathing [see page 143] and PC flexing, she claimed to reach "no hands" orgasms. If you want to try that, go to the Orgasm Loop—a better way because it incorporates that crucial psychological component—and eliminate the genital stimulation.

Frankly, I find trying to reach orgasm during masturbation without touching myself impossible. But I have interviewed women who are able to do it.

✳ Sex Envy

They were kissing with their tongues. That was obvious. One of his hands had disappeared up her skirt ten minutes ago. She was caressing the back of his neck with one hand—and who knew what with the other.

Feeling a little dizzy, Denise could not stop herself from watching that exhibitionistic couple making out at the end of the bar. They were in their forties—both in excellent physical shape, but still not young—and at least once a week they kissed and groped one another at *her* bar before heading out the door to a bed where no doubt they fucked their brains out. New Yorkers all have their neighborhood bars, the place where they stop for a quick drink and a shot of socializing before heading home. When Craig started working late every night, she fell into the habit of stopping by Olde Towne Bar after work for two glasses of white wine before going home to start dinner. And until that redheaded woman showed up, Denise was the queen of the regulars, all in their forties and mostly men.

And she had loved being the prom queen for the first time in her life.

"You look great tonight, Denise," Steve, the bartender said, openly ogling her cleavage. She'd started wearing push-up bras and low-cut T-shirts and sweaters beneath her conservative suit jackets after the redhead came along. *That* woman had cleavage. "They need an audience for their foreplay, don't they?" he said, gesturing at the couple, raising his eyebrows, acting offended, she suspected, strictly for her benefit.

Denise felt herself blushing from the bleached roots of her short blond hair down to her pedicured toes. What did they do in bed? Surely things that she and Craig had never tried, or maybe tried once and failed to pull off.

He was kissing the top of her cleavage now. She buried her face in his hair.

"They're ridiculous!" Denise snapped. Steve topped off her glass. She felt hot, feverish almost.

He nuzzled her neck, whispered something in her ear, got off his bar stool, and went to his knees before her. She gave him a wanton smile. He gently parted her knees with his hands and kissed the inside of each knee.

Denise gulped her wine, mumbled, "Put it on my tab," and rushed out the door.

Craig beat her home by a few minutes. He was in the kitchen opening a bottle of wine when she came in. "Great timing!" he called out.

"Hi, honey," she said.

Standing in the kitchen doorway, she watched her husband twist the corkscrew, mesmerized by his hands. They were long, slender, elegant hands. Suddenly his penis flashed into her mind. It was long, slender, and elegant too.

"Something wrong?" he asked curiously, handing her a glass of wine.

She was breathing heavily.

"Tired," she said.

He guided her into the living room. They sat down at opposite ends of the sofa. Impulsively she kicked off her shoes, put her legs up, her feet in his lap. He looked startled, but he set down his wine-glass and caressed her feet, massaging her insteps with those long, slender, elegant hands. She felt his penis stirring beneath her heels.

"We've never done it in here," she said.

"What?" He looked closely into her eyes. "Denise, how many wines did you have at Olde Towne?"

"We've never done it in here," she repeated. She felt her bosom heaving—yes, actually heaving. "Why not?"

"Denise . . ."

She got up on her knees, hiked her skirt, and straddled her husband's lap. He laughed nervously. She kissed him, fluttery little kisses full of passion as she unknotted his tie with trembling fingers.

"Denise," he said, but his tone had changed; his voice had grown thicker.

Awkwardly he fondled her breasts. She pulled back from him, took his hands in hers, and showed him how to cup and palm her breasts the way that man at the bar did it to the redhead. He groaned as she kissed him again, more sure of herself this time, her tongue licking his lips and the tip of his tongue. She felt his erection straining against his pants.

He moaned as she rocked back and forth on it. Reaching under her body, she unzipped his pants and pulled it out. The head glistened. She pushed her new silk G-string aside, rose up, and sat back down on him.

"Oh, God, Denise," he said, his breath, like hers, coming in heavy gasps.

He had never felt so big inside her, and she rode him to a stunning climax, rode him as surely as if she'd been riding like this for years.

Part V ....

RELEASE

"It's Over Too Fast."

Early ejaculation is typically a young man's problem. With age, men gain some control over the erectile process, and their arousal responses also slow down. Occasionally a man will continue to have this problem into middle age. In that case, he's probably not tried to correct it nor been with a woman who wanted to train him. He may have deep-seated guilt about sex. On the other hand, maybe he didn't outgrow the hurried and furtive masturbation patterns of his youth.

And some men don't have what they or their partners would describe as a "problem." ("Too fast" is a subjective judgment.) They just want intercourse to last longer. For them, some virtuoso tips are included.

The Standard Advice

Therapists suggest that he get treatment for his "issues."

Both sex therapists and sexperts pull out the standard bag of physical tricks: the squeeze technique; the stop-and-start method; continuing to pleasure her after he's finished.

The tricks do work. But you want more than that.

The Instant First-night Makeover: Planned Preliminary (Not Premature) Ejaculation

A man in his early thirties told me recently that he still masturbates to ejaculation before "the big date, usually the third date with a woman, the one where I know we're going to have sex. I want the intercourse to last long. So I jerk off before the date. That way I am relaxed and not desperate."

That is a good plan whether a man is dating or in a relationship or married. As long as he can have another erection and ejaculation later that evening, he can allay some of his performance anxiety by taking his private release early. For men over thirty-five, the plan is: Release in the morning before partner sex that night.

The Sex Life Makeover Plan

1. Engage in stop-and-start intercourse.

Men are conditioned to continue thrusting to ejaculation once intercourse begins. Break the conditioning!

After a brief period of thrusting, pull out. Continue stimulating her genitals with mouth and hand while she caresses or strokes nongenital areas of your body, like your back and chest. The more often you stop and start, the longer you will eventually be able to thrust without stopping.

2. Use the squeeze technique.

Developed from an ancient Chinese technique by Dr. William Masters in the early days of his pioneering sex therapy work, the squeeze is an oldie but goodie. It really works.

✳ Technique Tips ....

Pay close attention to his arousal level during intercourse. (And he should communicate that to you. This is a team effort.) When he is about ready to ejaculate, press his penis, just below the head, between your thumb and forefinger. Squeeze gently. After a few seconds let go. Rather than being painful, the squeeze releases pleasurable sensations that some men describe as a "preorgasm orgasm." In fact, he may want to delay orgasm two or three times before finally coming.

3. Try the testicle tug.

This is more effectively performed during manual or oral stimulation than intercourse. But it's a good technique for helping both partners learn about how he reacts when he is near his ejaculatory inevitability point, also known as the "point of no return." Once a man is there, nothing he or she does will stop him.

Technique Tips ....

Encircle his scrotum with thumb and fingers as he nears ejaculation. Squeeze firmly and pull down lightly. Hold for several seconds. This should delay his orgasms. However, if you squeeze too firmly or down too hard, you will cause pain.

Be careful with this one.

4. Adjust intercourse positions to put less friction on his penis.

The side-by-side positions naturally offer shallower penetration than missionary, female-superior, standing, sitting, or rear-entry positions do. But sometimes a small adjustment makes a big difference in any position. A pillow under the small of her back, for example, can change the angle of penetration in the missionary position. Speed and depth are critical factors too. Fast, deep thrusting encourages his orgasm. More shallow penetration, especially coupled with slower movement, enables him to thrust longer during intercourse before ejaculating.

A NEW MAN-ON-TOP

This intercourse position affords maximum sensation with minimal movement. That might help you sustain intercourse longer.

Have her lie on her stomach, legs straight out and spread only slightly. You lie over her, supporting your weight on your elbows. Position your legs on either side of hers. As you enter her, she closes her legs and crosses them at the ankles.

Crossing her ankles and holding her legs together enables her to feel the entire length of your penis inside her more intensely than she does in other positions. As you're thrusting, pay attention to her body by kissing her neck and back, nibbling her ears. She can reach under herself and stimulate her clitoris—in a position that gives her added stimulation.

It's an ideal intercourse position for the woman who says, "He comes too fast" and the man who argues, "She takes too long."

THE CHINESE WEDDING-NIGHT POSITION

According to legend, Chinese husbands in the period of the Ming Dynasty put their young virginal brides in this position so that the more shallow penetration would ease deflowering. She lies on her back with her hips at the edge of the bed, her legs hung over the sides, feet touching the

> *floor. He stands before her and leans into her between her parted legs.*
>
> THE FEMALE-SUPERIOR TWIST
>
> *This little adaptation of an old favorite puts a new spin on the concept of getting it her way. He lies on his back. She straddles him, facing his feet, not his head. He raises one leg, bent at the knee, foot on the bed. She angles her body so that she is riding his penis at the same time she is grinding her pelvis against his raised thigh.*
>
> *Slow motion for him—but double action for her.*

5. Make his ejaculation part of her sex play.

Allow him to ejaculate on your body as part of the sex play. He should continue pleasuring you with his tongue, hands, and vibrator after his orgasm. He will feel like a porn star executing the "money shot." And you might be surprised at how much fun it can be to take the hot semen and massage it into your nipples or inner thighs.

This feels naughty. Take early ejaculation out of the shameful category and put it under "naughty."

6. Learn two ancient Chinese techniques.

The Taoist erotic philosophy—not as well-known in the West as Tantra—places strong emphasis on regulating male ejaculation so that intercourse will last longer and women will receive greater pleasure. The keys to Taoist sex for men are withdrawal before ejaculation and controlling the pattern of thrusting during intercourse.

The basic withdrawal practice is called the "locking method."

✳ Technique Tips ··

When he feels very aroused during intercourse—but he has not reached the point of ejaculatory inevitability—he withdraws his penis so that only the head remains in her vagina. He remains motionless for ten to thirty seconds. Then he resumes thrusting slowly.

Taoist masters teach a variety of thrusting patterns. Try this simple one.

✳ Technique Tips ··

THE SET OF NINES

During intercourse, he performs nine shallow thrusts, then withdraws, pauses, enters her again, and performs eight shallow thrusts followed by one deep one. Again he withdraws, pauses, enters, performs seven shallow thrusts and two deep. The set continues in this manner until he takes nine deep strokes—which is supposed to bring her to orgasm.

> *Couples who have tried it report that varying the shallow and deep thrusts does prolong intercourse—though they typically lost count toward the end.*

What Sex Life Makeover Participants Say

A twenty-eight-year-old man: "We both love the money shot. It makes me feel like a porn star instead of a loser."

And from his girlfriend: "Before the makeover, he would roll away from me after his orgasm. I thought he was being selfish, but I figured out that he felt embarrassed and wasn't sure what to do to make it all up to me."

A twenty-three-year-old man: "The set of nines rocks. Really changed my life."

The Passion Flower Position

Several years ago the editors of Redbook *magazine asked me to develop a new sex position for their readers—a position that addressed some common concerns and complaints. The position had to: 1. provide the feeling of greater intimacy for her than the average intercourse position; 2. enable him to be both highly aroused and to sustain intercourse a little longer than he normally could; and 3. give them both exceptional orgasms.*

Working with a group of test couples, I developed the Passion Flower, an adaptation of the classic Yab-Yum position (see page 59). The reader response was gratifying. And I still teach this position to couples in search of something both hot and close.

ASSUME THE PASSION FLOWER POSITION

Sit in the center of your bed facing each other. Wrap her legs comfortably around his body so that she is sitting on his thighs. His legs can be splayed straight out or bent at the knees—whatever is more comfortable for him. Each places their right hand at the base of the other's neck and left hand at the base of the spine. Caress each other's necks. Stroke your partner's back, using upward strokes only. Look into each other's eyes and kiss with eyes open. Continue kissing and stroking until both are aroused.

Now insert his erect penis into her vagina so that the shaft exerts as much indirect pressure on her clitoris as possible. Rock together, slowly rubbing each other's backs now and kissing deeply with eyes open. Because of the intense clitoral stimulation the position provides, she should be able to reach orgasm this way, while the lack of deep thrusting helps him sustain intercourse without ejaculating.

After her first orgasm, they can move into one of the following variations:

1. He sits on the bed with his legs open wide. She lies back on the bed, facing him, with her body between his legs. He lifts her ankles up against his shoulders and enters her at a comfortable angle. She keeps her thighs

closed, creating a tighter grip on his penis. His turn to reach orgasm now—but she can probably have a second one in this position, especially if she stimulates her clitoris.

2. Or she lies on her back, again between his legs, but with her legs bent at the knees and pulled back against her body until her heels touch her thighs. He sits close to her with his penis opposite her vagina. She places her knees under his armpits and has him gently pull closer until he can comfortably insert his penis.

WHY THE PASSION FLOWER WORKS

The famed Bombay (Mumbai) sexologist Prokash Kothari, MD, taught me that there are three "feel-good" standards for any intercourse position: comfort, visual stimulation, and arousal, his and hers. According to the couples who tested the position and the subsequent Redbook readers, the Passion Flower meets all three criteria. And it satisfies her desire for emotional contact while enabling her to reach orgasm more quickly, while he can sustain intercourse without reaching orgasm so quickly.

WHAT THE COUPLES HAD TO SAY

"It definitely aids control because I couldn't thrust vigorously. I had to take my time and enjoy the ride. It's like having a built-in delay switch. I could enjoy her arousal and not worry about coming too soon."

And his partner said: "I felt very connected to him in

> *this position. And it stimulated my clitoris like inter-course never does otherwise."*
>
> *"The closeness is total," one man said. "We both felt our orgasms were more intense than usual. And I was grateful for the time it added to intercourse. I could feel and see her arousal building while I was still in control of my own. Brilliant."*

❄ The Panting Pussy

I always felt like I was letting her down. "Already?" she asked. Or she groaned and shut her eyes like she was fighting back tears. I felt like I was taking something away from her. No matter what I did with my hands and mouth later, I had disappointed her.

She began to seem to me like a panting pussy, demanding, ravenous, an animal I couldn't feed.

I wanted to make her squirm.

In the morning when she got out of the shower I knelt in front of her and sucked her pussy just long enough to get her hot. She left both a voice message and an e-mail telling me how much she couldn't wait for the day to end. She was home when I got there, mixing a pitcher of martinis. I know what she had in mind, and I'm sure she thought the alcohol would slow me down. "Want to?" she asked.

I pulled up her skirt and humped her against the wall. When she was hot, I told her I had some errands to run, picked my keys up off the kitchen counter, and went out the door. She called me on the cell phone before I turned off our street.

Two hours later I called her back. "I'm on my way home," I said. "Be naked when I get there." Five minutes later I called her again. "I'm pulling in the driveway. Get down on all fours."

She was naked and down on all fours in the living room. Her breasts were swaying slightly. Sweat beaded her upper lip. I took off my belt and swatted her lightly across the ass—twice.

"What do you think—" she protested.

"Shut up!" I said. I unzipped my pants and pulled out my erection. She looked at it hungrily. "Are you ready?" I asked her. She said that she was.

I shoved it in her mouth, shocking the hell out of her. But she sucked. When I was ready, I pulled out and shot my come on her face. She was shaking as she rolled over on her back.

"Rub it on your nipples," I said.

She did. I lay down beside her, put my hand in her pussy, and massaged the G-spot until she came, which was faster than I came, if she was keeping score. We rolled around on the floor until I was hard.

"Fuck me," she ordered.

And I did.

"I Don't Come with Him."

The woman in need of this Sex Life Makeover knows exactly what's wrong. Unlike a beauty-makeover candidate who's been wearing blue eye shadow and *Dynasty* hair for twenty years and can't see the problem, the woman who says, "I don't come with him" is clear on what needs a revamp. She is not having her orgasms when she most desires to have them—during intercourse.

And what a common female complaint that is!

Sometimes the plaintiff means: "I can't come with this particular man." In that case, if she's single, she might want to move on. If she's married or otherwise deeply committed to him, she needs to figure out why orgasms occurred in other men's beds, but not this man's. Can she rearrange the pillows to get into a more orgasm-friendly intercourse position? Can she subtly teach him the hand trick that old boyfriend (the one who clearly wasn't marriage material) used to make her come? Some adjustments can surely be made.

When they say, "I don't come with him," the overwhelming majority of women mean they can't reach orgasm during intercourse with *any* man. Yes, they come when he performs oral sex or manually stimulates them long enough. And, yes, they can come via masturbation.

The sex life problem area here is female orgasm. The makeover is not difficult, but she must take charge of it. Sound obvious? Getting her to take charge of her own Sex Life Makeover is the hard part.

The Standard Advice

Just as the women continue to ask the question, the experts still fail to answer it as clearly and concisely as they should. For example, before eventually informing his readers that most women do not reach orgasm via intercourse alone, Dr. John Grey of *Mars and Venus* fame says: "Orgasms are great—no argument there. But making orgasm the ultimate goal of sex is a guy thing. Most women care more about closeness, acceptance, and mutual pleasure."

And Dr. Judith Berman, of the attractive sex authority duo the Berman sisters, says: "For women, there are often psychological barriers to orgasm, including stress, and the pressure to 'perform,' especially if her partner is very disappointed when she doesn't reach orgasm." One could talk about those barriers for page after page, as, in fact, she and her sister do.

Women who rarely or never reach orgasm during intercourse are:

- reassured that they are the gender valuing "intimacy" over satisfaction;
- encouraged to seek individual counseling to remove their psychological blocks or couples counseling so they can build "intimacy" and talk about the orgasms she doesn't have;
- given pages of instruction on techniques for producing at least one, preferably many orgasms every time.

This is bad advice all around. I know I'm taking up more space refuting the standard advice than I have in other sections. That's because the myths and misconceptions are so pervasive that they must be not only addressed but also vigorously deconstructed. You're not having an orgasm during intercourse because of what you believe about how you *should* have orgasms—not because you're the intimacy-loving, never-mind-me fair sex.

After a few decades of interviewing women about their sex lives, I am no longer surprised at how many young, well-educated, otherwise savvy women really expect to reach orgasm on passion/love/whatever combination of the two. When it doesn't work out that way, they blame themselves and get therapy or blame him and maybe dump him, but they do not accept the situation as the result of anatomy and physiology, as they should. I am still surprised, however, that the expert advice isn't better than it is.

First, it's time we acknowledged how little the event of her orgasm has to do with him.

"If he were more skilled as a lover . . ." a dissatisfied woman might begin her lament. Yes, if he were a very good lover he would know that he must stimulate her clitoris during intercourse—and he would know how to make doing that feel like a natural part of his lovemaking. He would have a varied sexual repertoire that included this skill.

Never mind him and what he should/could do. She can have an orgasm with a mediocre lover if he's the man she wants in her life. Whether orgasms happen or not is more up to her than him. That's not a feminist or postfeminist statement. It has always been the truth for women.

Why?

One of the few irrefutable statistics in sex research—a field where similar studies get dissimilar results, like 10 percent of women cheat according to one study, while 50 percent do, says another—is this: *Less than a third of all women reach orgasm via intercourse alone.* They need additional clitoral stimulation to reach orgasm during intercourse. Sometimes the finger *is* mightier than the penis. Men may not want to acknowledge that fact, and women may fear bruising his "delicate" ego by mentioning it. Okay. Don't say anything. Get over the idea that you have to talk about your sexual needs with him in clinical detail. You can

get what you want and need without scheduling a sex talk.
Use simple physical gestures and take what belongs to you.

The Instant First-night Makeover: Stop Faking Orgasms!

This basic but crucial information about how women reach orgasm has been not only widely available but also very well publicized for decades. Yet women still ask advice columnists in magazines and on Web sites why they can't have an orgasm during intercourse. It is the number one sex advice Web site question—closely related to the answer women of all ages give in sex behavior surveys to that other question, "Do you fake orgasm?" Yes, women do. Up to 88 percent of women admit to having faked at least "occasionally."

Women fake orgasm because they think something is wrong with them or him when they don't come during intercourse.

Tonight, don't fake an orgasm: Have one.

✳ Technique Tips ....

MANUAL STIMULATION DURING INTERCOURSE

Here's how: Either you have to touch your clitoris and/or the surrounding tissue during intercourse or he does. One or the other need only insert a finger or two or the side of a hand between your bodies and stroke. If both are too squeamish for manual contact during the act, then he must arouse you to fever pitch via manual, oral, or a combination of both forms of stimulation before

> *penetration. In that case, you need to be on the verge of*
> *orgasm before intercourse, to the point where a little fric-*
> *tion anywhere in the genital area will trigger release.*
> *And—ta-da!—you will have that much-desired (and*
> *overvalued) "no hands" orgasm via intercourse alone.*

The Sex Life Makeover Plan

1. Masturbate before partner sex.

Some women are comfortable masturbating in front of their partners. If you are not a happy exhibitionist, whisper in his ear, "I need a few minutes to get ready," and go into the bedroom alone to masturbate. When you are highly aroused—on the verge of orgasm—call him into the room.

Could this be easier? If you are such a shy Alice that you don't want him to know you masturbate, slip into the bathroom, lock the door, and don't come out until you are hot. This is particularly effective if he has been complaining about the dearth of sex in your relationship. Men aren't surprised to find a woman suddenly very ready for sex. They are always finding themselves suddenly ready for sex. When they haven't had sex in a while, they will take it any way it comes to them, no questions asked.

SHY MASTURBATION

Use the palm of your hand. Press it against your clitoral area and move your body against it. You are humping your own hand.

Leave your panties on and use a towel. Hold one end with a hand in front of your body, straddle the towel, and hold the other end with a hand behind your body. Rub your towel back and forth. Ride it!

Hump your pillow. Lie on your stomach with a firm pillow wedged between your legs. Work your body against it as though you were on top having intercourse with your man.

Do it in the shower. Use a handheld shower nozzle and direct the pulsating spray to your clitoral region. This is very effective for many women.

Use a small, discreet, and quiet vibrator.

2. Show him how to masturbate you during sex play.

✳ Technique Tips ....

Put his hand where you need it to be. Keep your hand on top of his and teach him the strokes and the amount of pressure you use while masturbating alone. Don't turn this into a big sex lesson by talking about it; just do it. If

you're shy, keep your eyes closed and kiss him passion-
ately while he's learning your tricks. Don't let him move
to intercourse until you're near orgasm. Rule the action
with a firm hand.

You need not be an assertive woman to make this work.
Assertiveness is a quality required for asking him to listen
while you explain to him what you need to reach orgasm.
You need only be brave enough to move his hand around on
your body. If you're naked in bed with him, you should be
able to do that.

A man I interviewed for *What Men Want: Straight Talk
from Men About Sex* told me: "I really believe a woman has
sexual needs when she's reaching for me in bed, not when
she's setting up the lecture series to describe her needs to
me." Good line. I've never forgotten it.

3. Use your hands or teach him how to use his hands during intercourse in the most direct way possible.

✳ Technique Tips

THE FLYING V
*Many women find this simple move more effective for
inducing orgasm than stroking or circling the clitoris—
especially during intercourse, when the space available*

can limit the options. Insert the first two fingers of one hand between your bodies. Form an upside-down V shape with your fingers straddling your clitoris. Press the V in time with his thrusting.

Or take his fingers and place them in the V shape on the sides of your clitoris. (Picture his hand moving up your body the way your hand was moving down.) Grind against his fingers as he thrusts.

4. A no-hands orgasm (without preparatory masturbation) is possible if your PC muscles (see directions for Kegels on page 18) are strong *and* you get into the right position.

For most women the female-superior, or woman-on-top, position is most conducive to orgasm because she controls the angle and depth of penetration and can figure out a way to get the clitoral stimulation she needs.

❊ Technique Tips

THE OVAL TRACK

Use a sizzling move called the oval track that looks as good to him as it feels to you. Simply move in an oval track rather than a straightforward up-and-down pattern. Imagine you are circumscribing an oval with your body, with the downstroke at one end of the oval and the

> *upstroke at the other. Lean slightly forward as you push down on his penis, stimulating your clitoris. Pull up and move slightly backward on the upstroke, stimulating your G-spot.*

In any position, you can increase the odds of reaching orgasm by adding pillows, putting your legs around his waist or shoulders, or making other adjustments that create clitoral friction. On the downstroke, bump your clitoris against his pubic bone and grind. Again, strong PC muscles make the difference. If you flex them in time with the thrusts, you create additional stimulation to the area surrounding the clitoris.

❋ Technique Tips

THE CAT, OR COITAL ALIGNMENT TECHNIQUE
(SIMULTANEOUS ORGASM POSITION)

Sex experts have been saying for years that striving for a simultaneous orgasm with your partner is not realistic. They are certainly right about that! Some women, however, are desperate to achieve this. Often they are the same women who have difficulty reaching orgasm during intercourse at all. The CAT was developed by an American male psychotherapist to fulfill the desire of those women.

I almost never recommend a position or technique that I have not used to my satisfaction and/or that of my lovers. In this case, I make an exception because I've interviewed some women (and a few men) who embrace the CAT with such great enthusiasm. Try it. But don't blame me if you don't like it.

She lies on her back. He lies on top of her with his full weight so that, with his penis inside her, his pelvis is higher than hers. She wraps her legs around his thighs, resting her ankles on his calves.

This is key to success: They move pelvises only in a steady rhythm, which neither speeds up nor slows down until orgasm is achieved by both.

She leads on the upward stroke, pushing his pelvis backward while he simultaneously provides a counter-pressure on her clitoris with the shaft of his penis. He leads on the downward stroke, pushing her pelvis downward while she provides a resistant counterpressure by pressing her clitoris against the base of his penis.

I think this is a lot of work—not to mention smothering—to avoid one or the other of you touching her clitoris during intercourse, but some couples enjoy it, at least occasionally. "I love the intimacy," one woman said. "And it helps that my husband is not that heavy."

5. Cheat. Buy a tiny vibrator on a strap (or attach to a velvet rope or sew into a garter belt) and wear it during intercourse.

The Butterfly vibrator is small enough to fit between the two of you. Other discreet vibrators could be easily adapted to do the same job. You don't even have to visit a sex-toy shop. Quality products are available online. A bonus: He will enjoy the sensations too.

Not long ago women worried that their men might be "threatened" by the use of sex toys in the bedroom. Some men probably were. The cable channel HBO has single-handedly changed that attitude. Unless your guy is drawing a pension check, he will likely be titillated, not threatened, by a toy.

6. Separate intercourse and orgasm—at least for now.

Have intercourse in the usual way in one of your favorite positions. If you don't reach orgasm before he does, keep his semierect penis inside while one or both of you continue to stimulate your clitoris. It won't take long.

What Sex Life Makeover Participants Say

"In the beginning, we kissed, fondled, and rubbed against each other longer than we do now—which I realize gave me a lot of indirect clitoral attention. He was able to come twice or even three times in a lovemaking session. So I was getting a lot of stimulation. I would come during intercourse without touching myself or having him touch me. It didn't occur to me that I would need to do that when his sex pattern changed and he couldn't come two or three times in an evening."

From her husband: "When she indicated to me that she needed a helping hand, I felt like a bad lover. Why wasn't I doing it for her? Was my penis too small? Then I read up on the subject and realized she—and I—are normal. No big deal. I like playing with her pussy."

❈ The Story of No O

Angelina dreamed of being carried away on waves of passion—orgasms throbbing, blood pounding in her engorged vulva, limbs loose and trembling at last in sweet relief. Oh, Angelina, what a dreamer! In daydreams and night dreams, in vivid fantasies and snatches of remembered lips and hands barely glimpsed through the fog of sleep, she dreamed over and over again of reaching orgasm. The moment of ecstasy. The ultimate pleasure. The climax that would leave her sated.

In real life she slept in a bed of cold, hard frustration, her legs taut with muscle tension, her arms at her sides, carefully holding her body away from his. The only pounding she heard was the angry blood in her ears, the sound of passion rising and falling without resolution yet again. Sometimes as she fell asleep a tear or two would escape her eyes and trickle into those ears, making the sound echo like surf. Her face was set in the mask of an unsatisfied young wife, quietly resentful, deeply hurt.

Her husband, Jeff, slept beside her, spent, relaxed, apparently oblivious to her state of frustration. Either he bought her act of faked orgasm, or he chose to accept the performance, not really caring if she had come or not. Either way, she resented him. And she could not show that resentment in the morning when they bumped into each other as they each got ready for work, or in the evening when they prepared dinner together in the tiny space of their apartment kitchen, and certainly not at bedtime, when he would look at her breasts as though they were rich confections made for his appetite alone. "I want you," he would say.

Would she take him in her arms, faint hope stirring once again, or would she plead headache, PMS, stomachache, "early meeting, need my rest"? Her mother had lived like this. And probably her grandmother had lived like this.

Lying beside him, she longed for release. There was no privacy, no space, no time. She got to do it—masturbate—only when he worked late or went out with friends or she contrived to send him out on errands alone. She cast a sideways glance at him. He was handsome. Tall and lean, dark and brooding—he was, she thought, the man of her dreams when she met him three years ago.

Angelina did have orgasms with him then, not the first, but every second time. In the very early days before they married, he could get erect again almost immediately. They never made love just once, always twice. She was aroused the first time, thrilled with being taken as his hard penis, firmer than any flesh she'd felt before, claimed her wet, soft interior. Her body arched up against his. A shiny film of sweat covered her face as she faked those initial cries of pleasure. She was believable then because she was that wildly excited, barely able to control herself from pressing a hand into her vulva, thumb circling clitoris, bringing it out of her like a summer storm.

He owned her in those minutes they both waited for his penis to rise again. She did what he told her to do. "Take me in your mouth," he said; and hungrily she put her lips around the head, swirling it with her tongue. He moaned. She flicked her tongue back and forth across the ridge and he jolted to life in her hand. He roughly put his knee between her legs, took one nipple between his fingers, pinched it, pulled it out until she winced, then pushed it back against her breast. She would do anything he wanted, would have taken it up the ass, endured a whipping, sucked another man—or a woman!—while he watched. Anything. She wanted to feel his stiff penis inside her again, staying this time until she came, and she would pay any price for that.

One rainy afternoon when she was in this state in his bed, he put his hand between her legs and watched her gasp and writhe. "You are so hot," he said. "I've never known a woman this hot." His mouth replaced his fingers around her swollen organ. She grasped the brass headboard with both hands as he drew her orgasm out with long, slow strokes of his tongue. Before the contractions of her orgasm had ebbed, he thrust inside her. She came all over again with her trembling legs wrapped around his neck.

Aching with dissatisfaction now in her chilly marital bed, she recalled that day, lingered in her mind over every stroke he took inside her, each drop of sweat falling from his face onto her body, and especially the rolling waves of orgasms.

In the morning Angelina decided she could be late for work this one day. "I'm headachy," she told Jeff and then her boss on the phone. "It feels like the start of a sinus infection. I'm going to take a pill and a nap and come in around eleven." Jeff was solicitous, her boss understanding. She could not wait for Jeff to leave the apartment. He dallied over coffee, and she was tormented by the need to touch herself now. *Leave,* she silently beseeched him. *Leave.*

As he dawdled over organizing his briefcase, she ran through her list of favorite fantasies in her mind. She was serviced by two men and she returned the favor until her jaws ached, deeply grateful for the come they spilled into her mouth. A stranger who looked like Antonio Banderas bathed her in champagne and licked her clean until her throat was hoarse from crying out in pleasure. There was the beach seduction; another stranger encounter, this one on a train; and the cruel master who bound her to a chair.

Finally she was kissing Jeff good-bye at the door, her heart pounding, her nipples erect beneath the soft black satin robe. He held her face briefly in his hands, gave her a quizzical look, and left. She expelled her breath in a ragged sigh. *Now,* she thought, *now.*

Her fingers shook as she pushed her underwear aside in the drawer, and found and opened the antique box covered in faded burgundy silk, the box that held her small vibrators and lubricant. She poured a little of the liquid into her palm and swirled three fingers in it. When she shrugged out of her robe, she caught sight of her naked body, glistening palm of one hand and fingers of the other, and caught her breath. Nipples hard, chest flushed, eyes glazed. How long since Jeff had seen her like that?

Breathing hard, she lay back on the bed with knees bent. Her body jerked in a single spasm when she touched slick hand to clit. She wanted it, the orgasm, wanted Jeff to shove his knee between her legs and insist that she wait for his cock to fulfill her. Eyes shut, in a fever, she stroked herself faster and faster.

She felt Jeff in the room before she opened her eyes and saw him. He grabbed her hand and pulled it away from her body. She cried out. "Please," she said. "I need it. I have to come." He unzipped his pants, exposing his penis, as fine and hard as she'd ever seen it. Holding both wrists tight above her head, he stroked her first with his fingers until she thought she would go mad, then entered her, thrusting deep and slow. "Faster," she begged. "Please." He stopped. She thought she would die. He took one nipple in his mouth, sucked and nibbled while she moved her pelvis up and down, begging for him. "Not yet," he said. She couldn't breathe. He put his mouth on her vulva, licked her clitoris until she was almost there. And then he was on top of her, riding her joyously until she felt those waves of her dreams building from inside her body and breaking out, rushing over both of them, and leaving them exhausted in their wake.

After that day, Angelina didn't have to masturbate in secrecy anymore. And Jeff didn't hesitate to use his hands.

Part VI ....

ATTITUDE

"I Get Bored with a Woman After a Few Weeks/Months/Years."

Singles, particularly men in urban areas, are so good at keeping their options open, they don't know how or when to make a choice anymore. Internet dating has only compounded the situation. An attractive, successful man in his thirties recently told me, "There are so many beautiful, smart women in Manhattan. After I've dated a woman a few times, I can't stop myself from thinking, 'She's wonderful, but there's probably somebody better around the next corner.'"

These guys behave as though they all had their own reality bachelor shows—and in a way they do. But some of them eventually get tired of conquest sex with many new partners. They don't know how to have a sexual relationship with one woman when they are emotionally ready for it.

The Standard Advice

Therapy for him. Books like *The Rules* for her.

I despise books that tell women how to "catch" men. The man-as-big-fish concept denigrates both men and women. Landing him shouldn't be her life goal. If he can't commit or doesn't want to commit, she can't make him. And she shouldn't want to try.

If he *is* ready to be monogamous, however, this makeover can help him effect the transition from the guy who doesn't call when he says, "I'll call you" to somebody's boyfriend.

By the way, she might be the one who gets easily bored. Commitment phobia isn't limited to men anymore. Women too come home from dates with great guys to check for responses to their Match.com postings . . . just in case.

The Instant First-night Makeover: Spike the O

What can you do immediately to make the sexual experience so memorable that he (or she) won't be wondering if there's someone new on Match.com tomorrow? Spike the orgasm. Without using any special techniques that signal: *Hey, I'm going out of my way here to send you higher*, you make sure that his (or her) orgasm is a little more intense than usual.

The subtle tricks for her to use on him:

THE HIP ROCK 'N' ROLL

If he's on top and close to orgasm, grab his hip bones or buttocks and rock him, side to side or back and forth. When you control the direction of his pelvic movements, you also control the speed of thrusting and the depth of penetration. To him, it feels like you are pulling the orgasm out of him in a very explosive way.

If you're on top and he's close to orgasm, put your hands on his hips and pull him toward you. Keep your body weight on your knees so that you aren't bearing down on his hips. Again, he will feel like you're pulling that orgasm out of him.

And if you want to give him something really special, fellate him to orgasm. When he's near ejaculation, take his pelvis in both hands and rock him toward you so that he goes deeper into your mouth. And swallow.

THE NIPPLE PINCH (OR BITE)

Men who like having their nipples fondled also really enjoy having them pinched or bitten (lightly!) at the moment of orgasm.

THE PAUSE

If he's on top, grab his buttocks at the moment of orgasm, use your PC muscles to pull him in a little deeper, and make eye contact with him.

The subtle tricks for him to use on her:

✳ Technique Tips

THE NIPPLE PINCH (OR BITE)

If her nipples are particularly sensitive, she'll like this one too.

EYES-OPEN KISS

A tender, passionate—intimate—act. She will think you really care. Maybe you do.

TERMS OF ENDEARMENT

Some men whisper "Give it to me, baby." I like that because it makes me feel like my orgasm matters a great deal to them. Other women, however, might like, "Beautiful," or "You're beautiful." Say "I love you," if you mean it.

THE G-SPOT TWIST

If you are giving her an orgasm via cunnilingus, stimulate her G-spot at the same time. The orgasm will feel like it's coming from both places and crashing rapturously throughout her genitals.

The Sex Life Makeover Plan

1. Play games!

Easily bored partners need to create their own diversions with each other or they will be looking elsewhere for sexually challenging play. They are likely creative, assertive people who play a lot of games anyway. Role-playing isn't optional here. It's necessary.

Treat him badly and let him have makeup sex. Meet at a bar, pretend she is another woman, and have stranger sex. Agree not to see each other for a while and have desperately needy sex. Tease each other with stories about ex-lovers. (Other couples could not handle this, but you can. You crave it.)

2. Check out the boundaries.

Have you asked if she would do a threesome? Have anal sex? Go to a strip club with you? Take a strip class herself?

Have you asked if he would consent to being tied and teased? If he would spank you? If he would watch you have sex with another man or woman?

Sexual adventurers sometimes make the mistake of assuming that their partners are more conservative than they actually are. Never hurts to ask. Even talking about "taboo" sexual activities can add excitement to the relationship for the adventurous.

3. Stage virtuoso performances.

The easily bored; the "can't commit"; the "Is there someone better at the next social event/Web site/Starbucks?" man or woman really needs to explore, expand, and develop his or her sexual potential. That restless craving for the next big sexual experience will not be otherwise satisfied. You can't have fantastic sex with a string of strangers. Good sex, yes. But the kind of sex that leaves you feeling like nobody ever had sex like this before happens only with a frequent partner. Isn't that a reason for the two of you to become exceptional lovers together?

Long and happily divorced and never celibate, I would be the last person to say that you need to be married to have good sex. In fact, I believe—and there's a lot of evidence backing up the theory—that marriage may dull the erotic senses. (I am willing to concede that this is not true for all married couples, so please don't send hate mail.) Anyway, I'm not promoting marriage or even long-term monogamy when I say: Develop a regular thing with a compatible sex partner if you want to reach erotic heights. Risk forging an intimate connection with someone who can intuit and respond to and match your next bold move.

You're bored because you are really good at the basics and you are ready for a sexual liaison that takes you beyond all that. In addition to the suggested techniques below, try positions and techniques from other sections of the book.

❄Technique Tips

THE BUTTERFLY QUIVER

Any woman can feel like a sex goddess if she perfects this move. It couldn't be easier: Simply flex your PC muscles in time with his thrusting. When his erection is very hard, have him slow down and let you control the thrusting dynamics of intercourse.

His cooperation is important: the butterfly quiver is most effective when he doesn't thrust vigorously. For greater control, shift to the female-superior position if you aren't there already.

Now flex your PC muscles in a continuous pattern of tightening (as you pull him inside) and releasing (as you push him out), replicating the pattern of a butterfly's pulsating wings. Make the butterfly flutter as fast as you can as he nears ejaculation.

When you have developed strong PC muscles, you can make him feel as if the ejaculate is being pulled from his body, a thrill for both of you. Both your orgasms will be intense, often multiple—and amazing.

THE FIRE-BREATHING ORGASM

See page 143 for fire-breathing directions. During intercourse, flex your PC muscles in the same pattern as your perform your fire breath, squeezing as you inhale and releasing as you exhale. Start by flexing with the panting, then deep breathing, and finally fire breathing.

This may sound a little complicated, but it really isn't. Fire breathing becomes a reflex action after you've practiced it a half dozen times. Your orgasm will be stunning in its intensity.

KAREZZA

An Italian word that means "caress," karezza is a technique adapted from ancient erotic teachings. It prolongs intercourse and encourages extended orgasm. For the jaded sophisticate, it's a new way to make love.

> *Drastically limit his genital movement in either the female-superior or side-by-side position. He does not move inside her unless he becomes flaccid, and then he only executes a few shallow thrusts to revive his erection. But he can—and should!—stroke her breasts and clitoris.*
>
> *She is in charge of movement, including thrusting her hips against his or contracting her PC muscles around his penis.*
>
> *No matter how excited she gets, he thrusts only enough to sustain his erection.*
>
> *He holds their lovemaking embrace until she has achieved at least one and preferably more orgasms.*

4. Turn achieving orgasm into a personal Olympic event.

Why not go for multiple orgasms, extended orgasms, whole-body orgasms? For some people, the pressure would be too much. But you are not the average lover.

Multiple Orgasms

Physiologically, all women are capable of having multiple orgasms, though probably less than a third of women do have them—and even fewer than that have them on a regular basis. Unlike men, women don't need a refractory period to "recover" from orgasm in order to have another. If a woman wants to have multiples, she certainly can.

There are four types of multiple orgasms experienced by women. Each can be achieved via intercourse, oral, or man-

ual stimulation (including to the G-spot) or a combination 197
thereof. They are:

Attitude

COMPOUNDED SINGLE ORGASMS

Each orgasm is distinct, separated by sufficient time so that prior arousal and tension have substantially resolved between orgasms.

SEQUENTIAL MULTIPLES

Orgasms are fairly close together—anywhere from one to ten minutes apart—with little interruption in sexual stimulation or level of arousal.

SERIAL MULTIPLES

Orgasms are separated by seconds, or up to two minutes, with no—or barely any—interruption in stimulation or diminishment of arousal.

BLENDED MULTIPLES

A mix of two or more of the above types. Very often women who are multiply orgasmic experience more than one type of multiple orgasm during a lovemaking session.

You can encourage multiple orgasms by using the Orgasm Loop technique on page 61.

What about men?

Men cannot have multiple ejaculations within a span of a few minutes, but some men can have multiple orgasms in that time period. How? They experience the contractions of orgasm without ejaculating.

This is an esoteric technique, disparaged by some mainstream therapists and sexologists and not likely to be workable for very young men or for the man who only has occasional sex. Don't be discouraged if you can't make this happen. Here are the basics if you want to try:

✳Technique Tips

Learn to control the sphincter muscle by holding back your stool when you defecate and then letting it out.

To strengthen the PC muscles, practice Kegel exercises. (See page 18.)

When you feel you are about to ejaculate, attempt to hold it back. This may be very difficult, even a little painful, at first, but if you persevere, you will be able to delay ejaculation for several minutes. Practice while masturbating.

Without quite realizing how you did it, you will experience the contractions and pleasurable sensations of orgasm—without ejaculating.

Continued stimulation via intercourse, oral, or manual means will produce multiple orgasms without ejaculation.

Extended Orgasms

If you study Tantric sex, you will come across the concept of "sexual ecstasy" or "high sex." That simply means two things: extending the time that orgasm lasts and expanding orgasm beyond the genitals. Doing these things, of course, is not all that simple and takes a little practice. Learn how to extend your orgasms during masturbation.

✳Technique Tips

HIS EXTENDED ORGASM

Masturbate without ejaculating for as long as you can. Use the stop-and-start method, or change strokes when you feel ejaculation is imminent.

Count the contractions you experience during ejaculation, normally between three and eight. Note the level and order of intensity. Typically the strongest contraction will be the first one.

The next time you masturbate, again delay ejaculation as long as possible.

When you do ejaculate, flex your PC muscles. Then continue stimulating your penis very slowly while squeezing throughout the ejaculation—effectively pushing the sensations of orgasm on longer.

HER EXTENDED ORGASM

Masturbate in a comfortable position using the Orgasm Loop on page 61. Keep the arousal image and the fire breathing going continuously rather than stopping when orgasm begins so that your orgasm extends (and likely becomes multiples).

You can both use these techniques during lovemaking. Extended orgasms are more likely to occur when you have time for slow, languorous lovemaking—the kind of sex that keeps you feeling "on the verge" for a long time. One makeover participant described this as a "slowie, not a quickie."

✳ Technique Tips

KABBAZAH

An extended orgasm just for him, Kabbazah has long been a specialty of Asian, particularly Japanese, prostitutes. (I am referring here to professional courtesans, women who are well trained in the erotic arts and have chosen their career—not to the underage girls sold into sexual slavery or forced into it by economic conditions.) American soldiers in World War II and Vietnam discovered Kabbazah on R & R leaves. The discovery, however, was neither reported in the mainstream press nor immortalized in musicals like South Pacific.

The requirements for practicing the technique:

· *He must be in a relaxed and receptive state of mind and body. His passivity is crucial.*
· *She must have a talented vagina. A woman can't perform Kabbazah unless she has achieved mastery of her PC muscles through diligent practice of Kegels for at least a period of three weeks to a month.*

Some positions are better than others for Kabbazah. The female-superior or sitting positions work best for most couples. But do experiment.

She stimulates her partner until he is just erect, not highly aroused. Then she inserts his penis.

He does not move his penis at all. Never. Not once.

She also strives for no pelvic movement, confining all movement, or as much as possible, to her PC muscles.

They kiss and caress each other freely.

She flexes her PC muscles in varying patterns until she feels his penis throbbing—indicating an intense level of arousal—which should occur approximately ten to fifteen minutes into Kabbazah.

She times her contractions to the throbbing of his penis, clenching and releasing in time with him.

He will experience a longer, more intense orgasm than normal.

And, after his orgasm, she can flex her PC muscles like mad and have one of her own.

Occasionally an orgasm is both intense and diffuse. The tremors seem to radiate out from the genitals to the far reaches of the body's extremities. You feel it blowing out the top of your head and out through your toes.

Imagine orgasmic waves getting bigger and bigger as they wash over your body. You can make it happen.

HER WHOLE-BODY ORGASM

Masturbate in a comfortable position.

As soon as you become highly aroused, use your other hand to massage with light, shallow strokes your vulva, inner thighs, and groin. Imagine that you are spreading arousal throughout those areas. Continue the massage during your orgasm, imagining you are spreading the orgasm into your body.

Next time you masturbate, apply the Orgasm Loop technique and the manual spreading. Now apply the method in lovemaking.

HIS WHOLE-BODY ORGASM

You need strong PC muscles for this.

During masturbation (and later intercourse) stop thrusting when you feel ejaculation is imminent. Flex the PC muscles and hold to a count of nine. Or try flexing nine times in rapid succession instead of holding the count. Now resume thrusting.

In lovemaking, combine this method with alternating stimuli. Also, when you stop thrusting, pull your penis back to approximately one inch of penetration before you start the PC flex. This takes some practice—but it does work.

One makeover participant who doubted he could ever experience a whole-body orgasm said: "After practicing in masturbation and getting better orgasms but nothing like a

whole-body experience, I used the delaying tactics three
times during intercourse. I had an orgasm that rocked my
world—and hers. My hands and feet trembled. For a second
I thought I was in an earthquake."

5. Challenge each other emotionally as well as sexually.

There is an emotional component to orgasm. According
to Tantric belief, the soul of one lover flows into the soul of
the other during deep kissing. Whether you buy that or not,
you will surely acknowledge that heightened emotions intensify sexual experience. Don't be afraid to ask intimate
questions or make observations of each other. If nonin-
volvement is your style, you need to risk a degree of in-
volvement to up the sexual temperature.

People who experience whole-body orgasms inevitably
report feeling a strong emotional connection to their partner at the time.

Get there faster with the Tantric Yoga Kiss.

❊ Technique Tips

*Preferably in the Passion Flower, Yab-Yum, or other sit-
ting face-to-face intercourse position, the couple press
their foreheads together. They breathe into each other's
mouths. As he exhales, she inhales—and vice versa.*

*While being as still as possible without losing his erec-
tion, prolong the kiss for one to two minutes.*

6. If you are both acknowledging that it's a "relationship," consider going together to a workshop on sexual practices and techniques. You could make the reservation on the last day of your seven-day Sex Life Makeover—giving you an ongoing commitment to future great sex. Let's face it: You will always need more sexual excitement than the average couple.

Tantra workshops are popular with many sophisticated lovers who like the idea of a weekend in the woods combined with esoteric sex teachings. What is this thing called "Tantra"? It's an ancient Eastern Indian philosophy based on the principle that sexual energy is divine. Over five thousand years ago Indians revered sacred prostitutes who were the generous practitioners of the Tantric religion.

In the modern West, we have borrowed some of the techniques from Tantra to improve our sexual performances. When we say Tantra, we mean using breathing and PC-flexing techniques to prolong and heighten the arousal phase, intensifying the intimate connection through eyes-wide-open sex, and having more intense orgasms because of all that.

The best workshops acknowledge that their program is geared toward helping Western lovers have more intense sexual experiences. Avoid the gurus who babble endlessly about spirituality, unless you are looking for exactly that sort of thing. And don't trust anyone who says you can't gain the specific benefits of Tantra that you're after unless you spend thousands of dollars and a lot of time.

7. Incorporate sex toys into your sex play in unique and interesting ways.

You crave more sensation than the average person. Sex toys should be a part of your sex life. One vibrator is not enough. Buy an assortment of vibrators for him to use on her, for her to use on him. Fill your nightstand with flavored oils, body paints, honey dust.

✳ **Technique Tips** ···

Use a two-headed vibrator on her while performing cunnilingus. You will be stimulating her clitoris, vagina, and anus all at once.

Hold a vibrator under you chin while you are performing fellatio on him.

Experiment with attachments; for example, put a cup attachment on a basic coil vibrator to stimulate the head of his penis. Run a wand vibrator up and down the shaft.

Use an anal vibrator on him while you are performing fellatio on him. When he is ready to ejaculate, press his perineum with your thumb.

What Sex Life Makeover Participants Say

A thirty-nine-year-old man: "I didn't think one woman would satisfy me. She does. We keep going deeper into each other emotionally through the sexual exploration. One feeds off the other. It's intense."

And from his partner, a forty-five-year-old woman: "We both have thrill-seeking personalities. This is working for us because we're seeking the sexual thrills together."

A thirty-seven-year-old man new to the "concept of relationship" says: "In my experience women get cozy and the sex cools down in the third month. This woman is different. She is really into the concept of taking it to the limit."

✳ Staying On

Hamilton and Mariah dated for about six weeks in typical urban-dating fashion. They met at a party. He was drawn to her cleavage and her artsy lifestyle, she to his designer suit and his Wall Street demeanor. The Opposites-Attract card. They made out in the cab. On their first date she could barely restrain his physical advances. The first time they had sex, on the next date, he pushed unsuccessfully for anal sex. She didn't let him go there, but the sex was hard, hot, and fast—leaving her sore but thrillingly sated. After a few more dates, he calmed down, didn't call when he said he would, and was, she was sure, impassioned over someone else's cleavage and ass and, again no surprise, he disappeared from her life.

When they ran into each other at the greenmarket on a mild February Saturday morning, she asked, "What ever happened to you, anyway?"

His eyebrows shot up in surprise and he laughed.

"I thought I was too much man for you, baby," he teased.

"Oh, yeah? Is that why you said, 'I'll call you tomorrow' and didn't call?"

"I apologize for that," he said. "It was rude."

They exchanged life updates. She noticed him glancing at the

open collar of her coat, searching, she thought, for a glimpse of her breasts. His eyes darted from her eyes to other parts of her body, the way they had the night she met him. He was interested again. So was she. She caught his hand, impulsively brought it to her cheek, and said, "It's really good to see you again."

She accepted his invitation to brunch because . . . oh, why not? And that was surely the same spirit in which he extended it. Yet as they walked toward Tamarind, an Indian restaurant they both loved, she couldn't help thinking—wishing?—there were something more.

"Did you really think you were too much man for me?" she asked.

"You were trying to tame me, weren't you?"

"No, I was just trying to tell you that you weren't going to get anal sex anytime soon."

He laughed and pulled her to him, one arm around her shoulder. Yes, he was strong. Big, handsome, muscular—he was a lot of man, but not too much.

"I missed you," she said, realizing as she said it that it was true.

"I missed you too."

Over brunch, she flirted with him shamelessly, touching his hand, arm, face, knee, as she talked to him in that low, throaty voice she associated with arousal. He touched her back. When he brushed the hair off her forehead and kissed her softly there, she knew they were going to bed.

It was raining lightly when they left the restaurant fortified by mimosas. In a shared cab they made out as they had done in that cab some months before. She remembered how much she'd liked kissing him and how good his big hands felt cradling her face, touching her breasts. And he remembered how lovely those breasts were. She invited him upstairs. They kissed in the elevator, almost missing her floor.

Inside her apartment his hands caressing her breasts were so hot she felt as if they were molding the soft cashmere of her sweater to her body. She led him by the hand to her bedroom, where they turned from each other, almost shyly, to undress. But in bed the unexpected happened. He made love to her with exquisite tenderness and she feared that something had gone horribly wrong. Did she no longer arouse the sexual beast in him? At the moment of his orgasm, he looked into her eyes with such intensity, she thought that she would cry. Afterward he slept with his head on her breast for thirty minutes. She dozed off and on. When he woke, she felt shy and offered him the shower.

She got up, pulled on an ivory silk robe, and, with a feeling of sadness, realized that was indeed that. Something had happened between them. She didn't know what—but she was sure he would run from it.

In the living room they sat side by side, he fully dressed, she in the robe, and drank Australian Shiraz as they listened to a Ray Charles album. She thought they were making the nice good-bye they didn't have last time.

"No woman ever talked as straight to me as you did earlier," he said.

Suddenly he set down his glass and stroked her nipple through her robe with the back of one finger, knuckle to nail. She shivered. He slipped his hand inside the robe and with the palm of his hand massaged her breast. Her hands shook as she unbuttoned his shirt.

Eyes closed, she moved into his mouth, kissing the bottom lip with an intensity of longing she didn't know she felt.

Before she realized what was happening, he'd dropped to his knees between her legs. His fingers parted her labia. Then his tongue—hot, oh, God, so hot—ravished her clitoris. She grasped his head and ground her body against his tongue. He put two fingers inside her vagina and rimmed her anus with another one. The orgasm seemed to come from several places at once and completely overwhelmed her.

She hadn't recovered from it when he mounted her, filling her, possessing her, thrusting in deep, hard strokes. "I can't get enough of you," he said just before he came inside her. She couldn't get enough of him either.

As they lay panting in each other's arms, he said, "I want to do it again."

And she said, "I want to do everything with you."

She would never have believed it possible to find a man who could be that tender—and that passionate. But she had found him. All things were possible.

"I Keep Picking
Bad Lovers."

When a woman tells me that she and her husband rarely make love anymore or that he doesn't thrill or please her in bed or that the sex is boring and routine—I immediately understand why she wants to fix the problem. She's married to the man. They likely own property and have children—not to mention a history—together. And once upon a time there was magic between them. Understandably, she wants to recapture that magic and hold on to her home at the same time.

But when a single woman says, "He doesn't want to have sex with me" (a far more common complaint than you would guess) or, "He doesn't satisfy me," I often don't get it. Why does she want to stay? Why not find someone else?

Sadly, I've interviewed enough women to recognize the

main patterns. Some women always pick bad lovers or men who are good lovers when they make love but withhold sex more often than they make that love. These women invariably pick the same type of bad lover. And they are more invested in their rationales for why they've chosen these guys than they are in making changes that will positively improve their sex lives. I've seen women turn livid with rage when their rationales are questioned.

And yet they want to know: *What trick can I learn, perfume can I buy, words can I say to make everything wonderful in bed?*

The Standard Advice

From the therapists: Therapy, therapy, therapy.

The sexperts suggest everything from meeting him at the door naked and wrapped in saran wrap or naked and tied with a bow to making him jealous by flirting with other men in front of him. In other words, they treat his disinterest like a classic case of low desire or couple boredom. It's not that at all. Or they suggest that his poor erotic performance is something she can fix. Well, maybe—and maybe not. Or they suggest that she can cure his wandering eye with a combination of demands, threats, and sex tricks.

Oh, definitely not.

I say: Give this so-called relationship a time limit for repair. If you can't effect a Sex Life Makeover in one week, let him go. Why are you really holding on to him? Fear of being alone? Fear of rejection in the dating marketplace?

Reluctance to acknowledge another relationship "failure"? Just because he makes a lot of money or looks nice in suits or is a kind person in the rest of his life?

None of these are good reasons for lying naked beside a man who does not make you feel desired and who will not leave you feeling both sexually and psychologically satisfied should he deign to share his body with you.

The Instant First-night Makeover: The Sex Life Challenge

I have little faith in those commitment deadlines women are sometimes encouraged (by therapist/authors and magazine journalists) to issue their recalcitrant lovers. Surely every man who responded positively to such an ultimatum has already been profiled in *Marie Claire* or been the subject of a Lifetime channel made-for-TV movie. The gauntlet you are throwing down tonight is not of the type cast by the weepy but plucky and proud romantic heroine who already has put a sizable deposit on a big white gown.

Tell him: "Our sex life is not satisfactory for either one of us. I know I am not making you any happier than you are making me. Here are the problems as I perceive them."

List your complaints, ranging from his withholding to total disinterest in whether or not you are satisfied. Maybe he criticizes your body or your performance. Perhaps he wants to have sex only the one way you just don't like having it. Whatever the problems are, put them on the table. Tell him what needs of yours aren't being met. And be open and receptive to his comments and complaints.

Now ask him: "What do you think is the big problem? And how do you think we can fix it starting tonight—and within the next week?"

If he insists there is no problem—that you're crazy or the problem is all in your head or you're the problem—go straight to the end of this chapter to a section titled: "How to Spot a Better Lover Next Time."

But if he says, "Okay, what are we going to do about it?"—start with just having sex tonight, no pressure. (You probably haven't done it in a while, right?) Afterward, each of you make a list of what you'd like to be getting sexually that you're not. This is never going to work if all the complaints are yours. Open yourself up to what he has to say too. (Married women, this is good advice for you, too.)

The Sex Life Makeover Plan

1. Share your lists. Agree to cut them down to each of your three main factors for this week. (If you're still together next week, you can work on the fine-tuning.) Devise a lesson plan for each person.

For example, your list might be: "He isn't affectionate or communicative; he doesn't respond when I try to initiate sex; he doesn't seem completely involved when we do have sex."

His list might be: "She doesn't try to be sexy anymore; she is too demanding sexually; she isn't interested in doing what I would like to do in bed."

Tonight: Each pick a complaint and address that issue.

For example, he will be more affectionate and communicative while she will dress to arouse him. He wants black stockings and red high heels in bed? Give it to him. She wants to be held and stroked? Do it.

> ## ✳ Technique Tips
>
> ACT LIKE A PORN STAR
>
> *Act sexy and loving, even if you don't feel it. Go through the motions. For her, cream your body, put on the bustier, thrust your breasts out. And for him, kiss her passionately, tell her she's beautiful, hold her in your arms.*
>
> *Be aware of how your bodies look as you interact with each other. Don't be embarrassed about striking a pose or artfully arranging your limbs as if you really were on camera. Emote. Throw yourself into sex and see if the performance doesn't trigger real feelings and desires in you.*
>
> *Just don't fake orgasms. No more of that.*

2. Walk down erotic memory lane together.

Was the sex good when you first got together? Share your memories of that while sipping champagne and snuggling to music you both enjoy. Tell each other what was so good about that sex in intimate, juicy detail.

Play graphic show-and-tell.

I remember when you got down on your knees between my legs and first took my cock in your mouth. . . .

I remember when you put your hand up my skirt and inserted your fingers beneath the elastic of my panties and I was so hot and wet. . . .

Get really specific. Now act out your memories.

3. Pick a sexual activity out of a hat.

Each write three activities on separate pieces of paper. The other must agree that those are acceptable, even desirable activities. Put them in a hat or bowl. Shake. One of you close your eyes and pull out a slip of paper. Hand to the other.

That person initiates the sex play.

4. Perfect—or create—your signature sex move.

Maybe you both need a special move. Signature sex moves generally fall into these broad categories: steamy opening moves, hand moves, mouth moves, and intercourse moves. Lovers are often remembered by their special kiss or touch—or the way she undresses and he thrusts during intercourse.

This book is full of technique directions. Pick your category and find a move to call your own.

How to Spot a Better Lover Next Time

There are plenty of clues. You've chosen to ignore them because you were really looking for something else in a man: pain, humiliation, sadness, despair—whatever. That's all behind you now.

You can tell a man who will likely be good in bed by:

THE WAY HE EATS

Does he savor his food or merely wolf it down? Is he a rigid meat-and-potatoes guy or a man who experiments with exotic fare, appreciates spices, is willing to try your marinara sauce even though you don't make it like his mother did?

Maybe some finicky eaters are great lovers, but they are surely in the minority.

Some women say that the food litmus test is whether or not he shares the food on his plate in a restaurant. That's actually not a bad indicator of how generous he will be as a lover. Do you want to have sex with a man who jealously guards his fries?

THE WAY HE MOVES

Some men walk with natural grace. Some have an athletic stride. Others move in a sensual, sexual way. These are all good signs.

If the guy trips over his feet or yours, bumps into doors, knocks things off tables, think how he will botch a trip to your clitoris.

HOW HE TALKS

Does he talk too loudly? Mumble? Is his conversation focused on self, business, and self again?

You're looking for a man who can modulate his speaking voice, effectively whisper in your ear, and ask some questions about who you are—as well as listen to the answers.

HOW HE LOOKS INTO YOUR EYES

We give everything away through our eyes. Do his show amusement, desire, intelligence, sincere interest in you? Can he hold eye contact? Does he know how to flirt with his eyes?

HOW HE TOUCHES YOU

A man who has both a firm handshake and a good hug—for men friends too—is likely to be a good lover. When he takes your arm, puts his arm around your shoulder, places his hand at the small of your back, or holds your hand, does his touch feel warm, confident, comfortable? If he occasionally touches your hand or arm during conversation, he's really trying to connect with you.

When he holds you in a full embrace, do his hands caress your body? Does he sometimes hug you with his arms around your shoulders, pulling your body close against his—a very sexy hug? Some men don't know any embrace other than hands clasped around buttocks as they pull you close.

THE WAY HE KISSES

Ah, I am convinced that the way a man kisses defines the way he makes love. Anytime I've ever ignored the questions raised by a lackluster kiss or convinced myself that I could show him how to kiss me, I've been disappointed in the sex. (And that explains why it's been years since I went to bed with a man who can't kiss.)

I promise you this: If he shoves that tongue artlessly into

your mouth at the first opportunity, he will do the same thing with his penis.

PUTTING ON A CONDOM WITH YOUR MOUTH

Now that you're out there in the world again, you must practice safer sex. Condoms are not negotiable. This showy little trick is worth learning. And you will need to practice on a few condoms before you're ready to put one on a lovely erection.

Make sure your mouth is wet. And have a glass of water on the nightstand in case you need more lubrication. Once he has a satisfactory erection, open the condom. Mint-flavored is nice; condoms treated with spermicide will gag you. Be sure you select one with a reservoir tip.

Suck the tip end of the condom into your mouth, anchoring it against the roof of your mouth with your tongue. Now place the entire condom into your mouth. You should be holding it between your lips and your front teeth.

Picture the flat circle of the condom held between lips and teeth with the reservoir end still anchored by your tongue to the roof of your mouth.

Be sure the tip of the condom is flattened before you begin moving the condom down on his penis. Otherwise there could be air bubbles in the condom—causing potential breakage. You don't want that.

Now, you're ready to put that condom on. Hold the shaft of his penis just below the head in one hand and the base with the thumb and forefinger of the other hand. Place your mouth (with the condom in it) on the head of his penis. Immediately *slide your lips behind the ring of the condom. Press against the head of his penis with your lips.*

Keeping that tip end of the condom against the roof of your mouth and the circle outside your mouth and flat against your lips, firmly push the condom down over the head of his penis and the first inch or so of the shaft.

Use your hands to slide the rest of the condom down to the base of his penis.

❉ The Fling

When Catherine spotted him on a sultry August Saturday afternoon, he was perusing the travel section in her favorite bookstore café, Kramer's, in the Dupont Circle neighborhood of Washington, D.C. She admired his butt, high and firm, outlined in a pair of snug and faded black jeans. A full head of hair, medium build and height, light brown skin, his features an interplay of races—he was exactly her favorite physical type.

"I have to tell you how attractive you are," she said, coming up behind him.

He turned, sized her up immediately—red hair, green eyes, petite but full-breasted—smiled, and said, "Why don't you tell me over lunch? My name is Bruce."

It was her neighborhood, so she chose the restaurant, a Malaysian place with palm trees, an atmosphere conducive to nurturing lust. He told her a little about himself, but she wasn't listening very closely. She was lost in the small patch of chest hair above his open collar. He took her hand and simply held it. No finger or thumb running suggestively across the back of her hand. No intentions traced on her palm. But the heat traveled steadily like a high-voltage current between them.

When the check came, he insisted on paying—and wrote down her phone number with the same pen he'd used to sign the credit card receipt. Outside the restaurant, he took her hand again, as if to shake it, but he held on to it. She pulled him to her and kissed him, softly, fully on the lips. His face beginning to sweat, he held her.

She wanted him, purely wanted him, wanted him for the sex, nothing else. Catherine hadn't been with a man in a while, and she was more than ready to be with this man.

"Did you leave the AC running at home?" he teased; and she was glad she had worn new black lace bikini panties under her little black cotton skirt.

At her apartment, they undressed hurriedly and fell into a clumsy embrace and then into bed. They kissed deeply and grabbed hurried hot handfuls of each other. The sight of his hands on her pale skin aroused her almost as much as his touch. They were light and shadow intersecting, sending delicious shivers throughout her body. His knee parted her legs.

He lowered his head, his lips grazing her nipples and belly on his way down. With the tip of his tongue he teased her clitoris by making slow circles around it, his movements halting at first, as if he were searching for the right place. She liked it that he didn't know.

Pushing her hips higher, she thrust herself against his mouth and gyrated. She was totally exposed, yet not exposed at all; naked, but not known. She came in electric jolts, not waves, the sensations shooting out of her and into his mouth.

When he lifted his head, his mouth and chin were wet with her juices. A glistening trail led down his neck. His penis was hard, quivering in anticipation. She pulled him to her, breathing harder, as he plunged inside. This time the orgasm came in waves, splashing against the guttural sounds coming from his body as if against rocks. He knew her now.

"I want you again," he said.

And she knew this was not going to be a fling.

Part VII ....

VARIATIONS

✳ *fifteen* ....

"She/He Wants a Little Kink; I Don't."

Sex in America keeps getting kinkier.

Some social observers say kink was always happening behind closed doors and has simply come out of the closet in the last ten or more years. Others believe that the pornification of America has led many people to try what they see in videos, DVDs, and online. Whatever. If your experience of sex is limited to "vanilla" (i.e., traditional) activities, but you have a partner who wants to pour on some fudge sauce and whipped cream and make a sundae—you are not alone. Sometimes the partner pushing for a little bondage or S/M is the woman. We can be kinky too.

The longer a couple have been together, the more likely one of them will suggest that, satisfying as intercourse, oral, and manual stimulation are, there might be other things to do together. Kink is a natural sex life progression. If you've been afraid to walk on the wild side, fear no more.

The Standard Advice

Therapists tend to focus on the extremes—men with fetishes, women who really want to be hurt. They see the need for therapy in somebody's future if kink is on the menu. Sexperts suggest compromise: Try it once or agree to a reasonable facsimile of the desired act or practice, if not the real thing. They offer advice on how to play with sexual variations without being coercive or coerced.

That is fairly good advice. I think you should be willing to give kink a go. These games, however, do come with rules. Agree to your terms beforehand. Generally those terms will include: No real pain. No blood. No serious humiliation.

And if your man has a fetish, you aren't going to be happy with him unless you share, for example, his total erotic absorption in your feet. Rare is the fetishist who has been cured by therapy. If all he wants to do now is suck, kiss, and lick your toes, he isn't Sex Life Makeover material.

Most men would just like to suck your toes occasionally or have you wear your highest heels to bed now and then. That's a little kink. And a little kink is a good thing.

The Instant First-night Makeover: Playing Slave

You are committing to only a short game of master (or mistress) and slave. Agree to reasonable limits, like no real pain, nothing that leaves marks, or absolutely no personal chores performed in the name of kink. Set a time limit. And don't back out. Let the erotic humiliation begin.

The payoff for you at game's end should be stimulation to orgasm by whatever means the master or mistress deems appropriate.

❄ **Technique Tips** ....

Things to make your slave do; some suggestions to get you started:

Have him strip for you. Your clothes stay on. Make him touch your genitals without seeing them by insisting he can only put a hand up your skirt.

Order him to be a voyeur with his hands behind his back. Undress and masturbate as though you were alone.

Make her strip, then blindfold and handcuff her. Tie her to a straight-back chair or the bed. Tease her to the point of orgasm over and over again. Masturbate and ejaculate on her body. Now order her to masturbate, using your ejaculate as lubricant. Tell her she will be punished if she doesn't have an orgasm within five minutes.

After you're kinky for one week, if you're not aroused, your partner has to get that elsewhere or do without. You gave kink a fair trial. But you will almost surely be aroused by one of these activities, if not several. Getting past feeling silly is the obstacle for some people.

1. Your partner takes one turn at playing the dominant or submissive role she/he has requested of you.

"Switching" as it's called in S/M circles, is only fair play. Can you expect your partner to accept a spanking or play slave if you won't?

2. Bound for love.

Most people mean a game of "tie and tease" (see directions on page 75) when they say "bondage." Those interested in deeper bondage experiences can get guidance on products—including gags, ropes, rubber suits—books, videos, and DVDs from the reputable sex-toy stores, also online. Toys in Babeland and Good Vibrations are my favorite sources for sex-toy products and information.

3. Spank.

Light spanking has an almost universal appeal. See directions below.

4. Add toys and accessories.

Kink is all about dress-up and play toys. Aficionados use

nipple clamps, wear ridiculous clothing like bras with the nipples cut out, put studded collars on one another, and generally shake up the sexual status quo in many ways. Explore the options. Add at least one toy or outfit to your toy box, something to nestle against the vibrator.

5. Embrace porn.

Women like porn too. About half the sales and rentals of DVDs and videos are to women consumers. But women tend to use porn as a sex aide—to add spice and variety to the sex—while men tend to use porn as a masturbation aide. His stuff is rawer than hers. Frankly, she would be turned off, if not appalled, by much of it.

Let him have his masturbation porn. She should pick out the porn they share in the bedroom. Look for anything by Candida Royalle's Femme Productions and for films starring one of the Vivid Girls, including Jenna Jameson.

A Kink Primer

Kink covers a significant amount of territory, from a light spanking to heavy practices like extreme bondage or erotic body piercing. We are dealing with only light kink, the games couples play from time to time to increase arousal and make sex more interesting. (If you want to go farther than that, you need to consult other resources.) Most people have tried or would like to try one of these sexual variations.

SPANKING

What it is: Strokes applied to the buttocks, typically by hand. They can also be delivered by the back of a wooden hairbrush or paddle, a kitchen spatula, or other household implements. You can casually swat your partner during intercourse or turn him or her over your knee for an old-fashioned disciplinary session.

Why it appeals: The buttocks are not only sensitive to erotic stimuli but also designed to take more pressure than other body parts. A slap to the buttocks brings blood to the surface of the skin. You feel tingly. A well-timed and well-aimed slap also pushes the genitals more roughly together—and that feels good too.

And don't overlook the power-play aspect of this game. The spanker is playing a dominant role, the spankee a submissive one.

How to incorporate it into sex play: After arousing your partner with kissing, caressing, and oral and manual play, start with light strokes to the buttocks to prevent bruising. As she (or he) becomes more aroused, make the strokes a little harder. Gauge your partner's response and don't take it farther than she or he wants to go. Experiment with implements. A wooden brush or a plastic spatula will make a different sound than your hand does, and that alone is exciting.

But remember: It's harder to tell how much pain you're inflicting when you don't have your own smarting hand as a guide.

BONDAGE

What it is: Restraining a partner primarily by binding wrists, ankles, or both. In the typical scenarios, either she/he is in a sitting position leaning against the headboard with arms outstretched and hands cuffed to bedposts, or she/he is in the spread-eagle position, bound by wrists and ankles to the bed. You can also bind your partner to a straight-backed chair.

Use Velcro handcuffs, silk ties or scarves, fabric belts, and other soft items. No metal handcuffs.

Why it appeals: The bound person relinquishes both control and responsibility for sex. Her (or his) pleasure is in the other's hands. Many high-achieving, overstressed men and women find it thrilling to be in a position where they merely receive with no obligation to give or perform or produce.

How to incorporate it into sex play: Introduce the idea of bondage as a fantasy element. "I have fantasized tying you up," or "I have fantasized having you tie me up and tease me to the point where I can't take it anymore."

During passionate lovemaking, take your partner's wrists in your hand and hold them together above her (or his) head. Or, if you want to be bound, in the heat of passion put your arms over your head and hold on to the headboard.

Now that you've put the idea in her (his) mind, ask.

LIGHT S/M

What it is: S/M is a power exchange between consenting partners with one partner playing the dominant role to the other's submissive. It's acted out through mutually agreeable games with clear limits. He may, for example, like to be verbally humiliated and "made" to get down on his knees and beg for sex. She may, for example, want to be bound and lightly whipped. There are endless scenarios, many incorporating bondage and the use of sex toys.

Toys include all manner of whips and floggers, most relatively harmless. Check out sex-toy shops, including online. Clothing is often a key part of the S/M experience, with leather, rubber, or vinyl items, high-heeled shoes and boots, and corsets as well as masks being typical accoutrements.

Why it appeals: Some people enjoy surrendering power now and then. Others enjoy assuming all the power. For some people, light S/M represents an erotic challenge. They take their personal erotic experience and the sexual relationship to a new level through games that test them and their partners to some extent. S/M allows others to act out repressed feelings of guilt or shame about their sexuality in a safe and healthy way.

And for some couples, S/M is something new and different, appealing in the same way that a new cuisine or type of music might be. They need a lot of stimulation and variety in their lives.

How to incorporate it into sex play: Start with love bites, slaps, and pinches. Hold her (his) nipples between your teeth and bite down gently. Administer little biting kisses to the inner thighs. Introduce spanking and light bondage.

If these various forms of rough play meet with enthusiastic acceptance, rent a video or DVD featuring S/M. Start a dialogue with your partner. Go online together and check out sex toys and erotic clothing. Visit a sex-toy shop. Come up with a scenario that you would like to act out together. Set limits. Create a "safe word," a word other than no that means you or your partner really does want to stop now. The word should be something you wouldn't normally say during sex, like elephant.

S/M may not be a game you play often, but it can add a kind of excitement to your sex life that you won't get any other way.

ROLE-PLAYING

What it is: A part of S/M but not limited to those games, role-playing does not necessarily involve bondage, discipline, or pain. It is all about acting a part. The couple in the popular yogurt commercial—she's the French maid; he's the wealthy employer—are role-playing as, dressed in her little uniform, she sits on his lap feeding him spoonfuls of yogurt and making suggestive comments. Couples who pretend to be strangers meeting in a bar are also role-playing.

Why it appeals: Acting a part frees us to step outside our own skins. We aren't restricted by how we define ourselves and our partners—and vice versa. Some people feel sexually liberated when they take off their business suits. Other people need to take off more than that occasionally to be free enough to play or experiment sexually.

How to incorporate it into sex play: Start by having sex outside the bedroom. Doing it on the living room floor or in the office after hours or in the backseat of the car (even if it is parked in the garage with the baby monitor in the front seat) can make you feel younger, bolder, more open to erotic possibility. Then suggest to your partner that you make a date with each other as strangers who met online. Play your roles throughout the evening and see where that takes you.

ANAL SEX

What it is: Anal play—with one or two fingers inserted into his or her anus—or annilingus—tonguing the anus— can be part of anal sex. But intercourse, with his penis inserted into her anus instead of her vagina, is the main act. She can use a strap-on dildo and penetrate his anus too.

Why it appeals: Receiving anal sex is the ultimate submissive act. Playing the submissive or dominant role is very exciting to many people. Anal sex is still considered somewhat taboo, a thrilling connotation. Most men enjoy the tight fit. Some women enjoy the stimulation, especially combined with manual clitoral stimulation.

It's hot or it's not. There's very little middle ground on anal sex.

How to incorporate it into sex play: See page 244 for directions. Anal sex requires both consent and preparation. If you're one of those guys who think you can just "slip it in," you're wrong.

VOYEURISM/EXHIBITIONISM

What it is: Voyeurs like to watch, and exhibitionists like to be watched. There is a little exhibitionist in most of us. Women who flaunt their cleavage are exhibitionists. Couples who make out in bars are exhibitionists—and the people watching every kiss and touch are voyeurs.

Why it appeals: Showing or doing something a little private in a public space is exhilarating. So is sneaking a peek at something you weren't meant—or don't feel entitled—to see. Obviously those creepy guys in raincoats who expose their pathetic penises have taken the concept too far.

How to incorporate it into sex play: Stop avoiding PDAs (public displays of affection). In fact, try turning up the heat on them. Touch each other in barely legal places, especially in dark bars. See if that doesn't have a positive effect on your sex life.

And ladies, show some cleavage or a nice expanse of stockinged thigh when you meet him for dinner. Get there early and make eye contact with the other men who are suddenly in your thrall. You will be surprised at how different you feel when you display your breasts as though you were a Hollywood actress on the red carpet.

As a woman who is not shy about displaying her assets, I promise you: Cleavage and bare legs will improve your sex life.

THREESOMES/GROUP SEX

What it is: It is exactly what it sounds like: three or more people having sex together.

Why it appeals: Threesomes are a safe way for a bisexual partner to explore the other option while including the beloved. It's not cheating, they reason, if she/he is part of the sex. Group sex or "swapping" serves the same purpose for straight (or gay or bi) partners looking for experimentation with minimal risk.

And some couples want to try a threesome because they've seen so many of them in porn films.

How to incorporate it into lovemaking: Introduce the concept as a fantasy element. Suggest making a list of people whom you and your partner might want to include in sex play. If you live in a major urban area, you can probably find a club or social group where swinging and/or group sex is happening. Check it out.

✳ *The Belt*

Lisa dreamed about the belt.

In her dreams, she begins lubricating at the sound of the rich leather belt being pulled through its loops. Tremors run through her body as he tests the belt against his hand. Thwack! She is tied to the bed facedown, spread-eagle. The first strokes are soft, almost caressing whacks of the belt, because he knows how to make her crave the pain. The sound changes as the strokes grow harder. Her body is covered in slick sweat now. And the belt hits with a wet thud. . . .

The dream always ended the same way, in orgasm. She woke with her hand in her pussy, panting and sweating, the stings she had dreamed disappearing as the contractions of her orgasm ebbed away.

Beside her Brian snored, sleeping soundly, unaware.

Sometimes she taunted him, but he didn't seem to get her point. "Spank me! You don't like what I said? Make me take it back!" He laughed. Or she picked up his pants discarded on the bedroom floor, slowly removed the belt from its loops, and lightly struck the palm of her hand with it. Once. Twice. He looked up, frowned quizzically at her, and maybe said, "Okay, I should pick up my own clothes. . . . I know that."

They'd been together seven years—and she had the itch to have her ass smacked with his belt. She'd had that craving for as long as she could remember. The dream about the belt had been recurring since she was a teenager. And why? Her parents didn't even spank her with an open hand, much less a belt.

She wanted that and she didn't know why. And she certainly didn't know how to ask for it.

The days went by. She didn't think about the belt until she dreamed it. Then she couldn't think about anything else for a while.

One night she woke before the orgasm started. Hot, wet, unbearably in need, she rolled over, took Brian in her hands, and climbed on top of him as he came to life. He moaned, barely opened his eyes, but thrust energetically up to meet her. She rode him to a furious climax, the belt hitting her rhythmically in her mind.

"What was that all about last night?" he teased her in the morning. They were jostling for space in the bathroom, getting ready for work. "Not that I didn't enjoy it! Wow! You were on fire!"

"I had a dream," she said.

"A dream," he mused. "Well, if it got you that hot, I hope I was in it."

Ignoring the inquiring look in his eye, she hurried out the door.

Several days later they were sitting on floor pillows drinking red wine in front of a splendid fire, and he said, "It's another man, isn't it? You're dreaming about another man."

"What?"

"That dream . . . the one that woke you. When you climbed on me, were you dreaming about someone else?"

Her face felt hot, maybe from the fire; maybe she was blushing. Stricken, she looked hard into her husband's eyes. He was hurt, confused. She had to say something, but she choked on the words bringing them out.

"It was a belt," she said. "Your belt."

"A belt?"

And she watched him figure it out, slowly, the thought process excruciating. She could see him remembering: "Spank me"; hitting her hand with his belt. He was getting it. And she waited for the look of shock and revulsion she expected to cross his face, crease his handsome features, cut him off from her.

"A belt."

She was hot with shame, with desire.

"A belt," he said again, his voice stronger, more confident.

He pulled her into his arms, kissed her roughly, whispered in her ear, "You want the belt," a statement, not a question. She trembled in response. "Take off your pants," he said. "Roll over."

Lying over the pillows, her ass quivering in the air, she received the belt.

"He's Not Putting It *There*."

He's a man—and he wants to go there.

Heterosexual anal sex is much more commonly practiced now than it was even a decade ago. The pervasive influence of porn—where anal sex is a standard sex practice—has doubtless contributed to the new status quo. Some women hate it. Some women love it. But most women will tolerate it sometimes for the right guy. In an ongoing relationship, it's hard to say "no" without agreeing to try just once—and trying even once can transform the relationship, because men love anal sex. And, if you're going to try it, why not do so with an open mind and a good set of directions?

The sexperts say: Don't pressure her into doing anything she doesn't want to do, especially this. And that's good advice—as far as it goes.

Almost no one will tell you: Do it more than once with him. Really get the hang of it before saying you don't like it. But I'm telling you that. Yes, it will hurt a little. Yes, it is a submissive act. You may not like it at all, but you can't fairly say that after one experience. Or you may discover, as I did, that anal sex with the right man at the right moment is an intensely erotic experience leading to astonishing orgasms. Like caviar and anchovies, anal sex is not an everyday experience—at least not for me, nor, I suspect, for most women who do like it.

There is an important caveat: You should have anal sex only with a regular, monogamous partner. Commitments have been made. STD test results have been satisfying. There is greater risk of HIV transmission anally than vaginally because anal tissues are more likely to tear than vaginal tissues. And HIV is transmitted blood-to-blood or semen-to-blood. If the skin breaks, the opening for transmission is there.

I am not encouraging anal sex with a man you barely know. Urban women in their twenties tell me that men are asking for anal sex on the first date. Absolutely not! This is special sex with the special man.

The Instant First-night Makeover:
Simulated Anal Intercourse

Promise him that you will accept anal penetration by the end of the week—with the proviso that you don't have to do it more than two (three?) more times if you truly hate it.

Promise her that you will go slowly when she does let you in there. "Slow and easy" is the most important technical direction in anal intercourse. If you push too hard or try to enter her too fast, you can cause pain, even bleeding. And I can safely promise you that you won't get another chance for years, if ever, should you do that.

Now that the promises have been made, tonight is all about anticipation and fantasy, not the real thing. In the rear-entry position, insert his penis into her vagina. The angle of penetration and the view of her buttocks—combined with the knowledge that he will get in there within a matter of days—make this hot.

She can make it even hotter by talking through an anal-sex scenario. Borrow one from a book if necessary. Make it graphic.

While she's talking and he's thrusting, he can play with her anus by circling a well-lubricated finger around the rim of her anus and, if she is willing, gently inserting one finger (angled slightly upward, the direction the rectum turns) inside as she nears orgasm.

1. Bring in the toys, fingers, and tongues.

On night two, still no anal penetration by his penis. He can arouse her by stroking the sensitive tissues surrounding the rectum with fingers and tongue (analingus) and by inserting one, then two well-lubricated fingers. Toys that can be included in the play session include anal vibrators (or anal attachments to vibrators), vibrating butt plugs, and anal beads—firm rubber beads on a flexible stem for insertion and removal.

The goals: to give her anal pleasure and to prepare her anus for penetration next time.

❋Technique Tips ....

ANAL MASSAGE

Massage her buttocks using firm strokes. Then use light teasing strokes—even gentle pinching—down the crack between her cheeks.

Separating the buttocks slightly, massage the innermost parts with somewhat less firm strokes than you used on the outer buttocks.

Apply the light, teasing strokes you used in her crack down to her anus. With a well-oiled finger, circle the anal opening lightly.

Using long strokes, begin massaging her buttocks

again, starting at the base of the spine and continuing down the perineum.

Massage her perineum with your thumb or finger pad, exerting light pressure.

Put your finger in her anus and gently circle inside the opening. Now add a second finger. Rub them in and out in simulated intercourse.

(She can do this to him too.)

2. Take the plunge.

✳ Technique Tips

ANAL INTERCOURSE

Sex play should include cunnilingus and manual stimulation of her clitoris as well as the G-spot and the anus. The goal: intense arousal before you begin.

She assumes a comfortable position. For many women the rear-entry position with chest flat on the bed and ass elevated is the best position. There are other options; for example, she can lie on her back with legs straight up or ankles resting on his shoulders while he kneels between her legs and enters her.

Always use a specially designed anal condom and plenty of lubricant, like Astroglide. (No scented lotions or petroleum jelly, which can damage condoms.) The con-

dom is essential to keep bacteria out of his urethra. Using his fingers (protected by disposable finger cots if he plans to touch her vaginal area afterward), he generously lubes her anus and inside her rectum. She should find this pleasurable.

Start very slowly. As he presses the head of his penis against her anus, she relaxes the sphincter muscles in her rectum. He should not force his penis into her. Instead, she bears down on the head of his penis until he is past the sphincter muscles.

Now he thrusts slowly and carefully, following her lead. She controls the depth and speed of penetration. While he is thrusting, she or he—if his fingers are clean— strokes her clitoris.

With any luck, you will both reach orgasm.

Afterward, he must not insert his penis (or fingers) into her vagina until he has disposed of the condom and washed his hands. You both risk contracting a urinary tract infection from anal sex if the cleanliness rules are not followed scrupulously. No vaginal sex after anal sex until he has thoroughly cleaned up.

3. Now just do him.

A clerk in one of the Manhattan Toys in Babeland stores told me: "Almost every day a woman comes in specifically to buy a strap-on dildo so she can anally penetrate her straight male partner. A lot of them have seen the 'Bend Over Boyfriend' videos, of course."

Whatever the inspiration, heterosexual couples are practicing anal sex—with him as the receiver—in growing numbers. Whether he is enthusiastic about the concept or not, he has to receive anal sex one night this week after you have given so generously of your ass to him. It's only fair.

Use the same oral and manual anal techniques on him as he used on you. Bring out the beads and anal vibrator. Strap-on or not? Your call. He will, of course, receive whatever you wish to give.

What Sex Life Makeover Participants Say

"My husband was obsessed with getting me to do anal sex. We had tried it once. It hurt and I cried. Using the makeover directions, we were able to do it without so much pain. I can't say it's my favorite thing, but I will do it for him now and then. And he is so grateful!"

But another woman says: "Anal sex hits my G-spot. I play with my clit while he fucks my ass. It's amazing." She adds, "I have penetrated him with a strap-on dildo. I felt very empowered. He wasn't quite as thrilled with the experience as I was."

But her boyfriend says: "It's taboo. That alone makes it worth doing."

❋ *Surrendering*

Wendy held a butt plug in the palm of her hand. About two inches in length and less than that in diameter, the plug was designed with a flat base. And she couldn't help thinking that base was meant to keep the damned thing from getting lost up her intestines. Staring at it, she shivered. Her breath came a little faster just thinking about what would happen later tonight.

"You're really going to let me in there?" Ryan had said, his hands kneading the flesh of her buttocks. "Really?"

She took off her panties, lubricated the plug, and worked it into her asshole. *Ouch!* Resting both hands on the bathroom counter, she leaned forward, adjusting to the sensation. The woman at Toys in Babeland told her, "The plug opens you up a little bit and gets you used to the idea of anal penetration." Oh, yeah, like she would ever get used to that.

In a few hours Ryan's cock would be penetrating her asshole. She was obsessing on the pain to come, had been obsessing on that pain all day. "You want it," he said. Not just, "I want it." But, "You want it." When he said that, she knew he was right. She did. But she couldn't stop obsessing on the pain.

She walked around the apartment, straightening up, watering plants, with the plug in her ass, her panties off.

"How does it feel?" Ryan asked. He was calling from his cell phone, stuck in traffic. "How do you feel?"

"Submissive," she said.

"That's good," he said. He was laughing when the traffic moved and he drove into the hills where she always lost him.

She took out the plug just before he got home. He strode in like a conquering hero. "I love your ass," he said.

Yeah, but is my ass gonna love you? she thought.

His hands cupped her buttocks as he pulled her close in a passionate embrace. In erotic fury, they groped each other, pushing tongues into mouths, pulling flesh into hot hands, licking each other like animals in heat. He leaned her against the wall. She wrapped one leg around him. And they dry-humped until she almost came. Abruptly, he pushed her away.

"Now," he said.

Now. He took her hand and led her to the bedroom. The anal condoms and lube were in a basket on the nightstand. Candlelight filled the room with a soft glow. Incense burned. Her heart fluttering girlishly in her chest, she felt like the sacrificial virgin. He popped the champagne that had been chilling in a bucket of ice and poured flutes for both of them. She gulped hers before stripping down and assuming the position, facedown, her chest on the bed, her ass elevated by pillows.

He knelt between her legs and began licking from the inside of her knees up her inner thighs—broad, hot, wet strokes. His tongue worked its way to her clitoris and ran rapid circles around it. She wanted to come but he wouldn't let her. His tongue rimmed her anus. Lubricated fingers followed.

And then the head of his penis was pushing at her back door.

"Bear down," he whispered.

She did as she was told, pushing herself against his erection until she felt it enter this most private part of her body. Breathing deeply and rhythmically, she forced herself to move with him as he thrust into her. His cock—hard, hot, searing—sought out places in-

side her that had never been touched. After the first pain subsided,
she eagerly gave those parts. She opened herself completely to
him.

He took her hand and put it to her clit. She stroked in time with
his thrusts. When she came, she saw stars on a background of red.

"We Never Have Sex Because We Can't Ever Agree on When, How, or How Much."

What is a nice little chapter like this one doing amidst anal sex and kink? Doesn't it belong with "too tired, too stressed" or "thrill gone"?

No. This is all about power—and about couples who use sex as a weapon or withhold it as means of handing down discipline and maintaining control. This is not really a nice little chapter at all. That couple with the whips are much kinder to each other than you two are.

You may say, "The sex was good and now it's bad."

Or you may say, "We never had good sex and I only married him (her) because . . . *(she was pregnant, I was pregnant, I was broke, weak, vulnerable, young, stupid. . . .)*"

It doesn't matter what you say. Your excuses, rationales, and defenses *are* your sex life. Enjoying that, are you?

The Standard Advice

The experts say: Therapy. Compromise. Rev up the understanding and acceptance quotients.

They dwell on the minutiae, giving advice like, "Negotiate timing. If he is a morning person and you are a night person, sneak away from your offices for nooners in the Kmart parking lot." Oh, yeah. That's going to solve your problems.

Your problem is not timing, disparate levels of desire, or a disagreement over how many times a week you're going to do it to each other. Those are the symptoms of your problem, your excuses. You are both angry—and that's your problem.

Therapy can be useful for figuring out what happened. That can take a while. Meanwhile, start having sex again—good sex. Get over the idea that you can't have good sex with someone you currently loathe. Of course you can. Who over the age of twenty-five hasn't?

Sex connects people. If you want to stay with your partner, you must have regular sex—or work out a civilized agreement in which you are both free to have sex with other people while maintaining the corporation that is the marriage. This American habit of living in the sexless marriage/relationship (without seeking outside release) is ugly.

You will have sex tonight. He is responsible for his erection. She is responsible for her own orgasm if she wants to have one.

Set a timer and allow five minutes each for manual pleasuring of him, then her, oral pleasuring of him, then her, and five minutes of free-form sex play. Now have intercourse in the missionary position for three minutes. Switch to the female-superior position.

Sex ends when one person reaches orgasm—or both agree they're too tired to go on. The person who came might generously offer to bring the other to climax.

How hard was that?

The Sex Life Makeover Plan

In fact, there will be no-excuses sex for the rest of the week. You will have sex at least two additional nights this week, and preferably three, regardless of life circumstances. Tired, busy, "not in the mood," headache—any and all excuses are not acceptable.

1. Make a dramatic physical change in your erotic appearance.

Sometimes a new look can trick your—and your partner's—mind in a good way. Here are some easy and sexy physical changes:

GET DESIGNER PUBIC HAIR

Have you noticed at the gym that women over thirty-five or forty have bushy pubic hair, while younger women have none or neatly shaped little patches? Wax, shave, or trim that hair if you haven't already—and considering the state of your sex life, I'm guessing, no matter your age, you haven't already.

Men can shave or trim too, by the way. The wax seems a little tough for the typical delicate male, doesn't it?

LINGERIE!

It's the oldest trick in the book, but it always works. Sexy lingerie—the quality stuff, not the cheap crotchless panties in neon colors—makes her feel sexier and turns him on. All the physical changes are a two-edged sword: You feel sexier and your partner perceives you as more erotically appealing too.

GET A BEAUTY MAKEOVER

Him too. And both of you: Dress better around the house. Loungewear can be sexy and comfortable.

DO THE OBVIOUS.

Vacuum wearing nothing but a man's white shirt and bend over a lot. (He can do this too.) Unbutton those blouse and shirt buttons, exposing cleavage or chest hair. (If you have both, don't unbutton.) Tease. (See page 93.)

2. It's all about her.

Ask her how she wants to reach orgasm and how many she wants to have. Directions for manual stimulation are on pages 90–92, cunnilingus on page 113. If she wants to reach orgasm during intercourse, see pages 173 and 176.

Forget about yourself tonight. Your job is to please her. It does not matter if you achieve a full erection—as long as you can sustain intercourse if she desires that—or reach orgasm.

3. It's all about him.

Ask him how he wants to reach orgasm. Directions for a hand job are on page 56 and a blow job on page 121. Assume any intercourse position he requests.

This is not your night. If you enjoy it, fine. And if you don't, that's fine too.

What Sex Life Makeover Participants Say

"Well, it annoyed the hell out of me to be told that my excuses for why we didn't have sex were camouflage for anger and resentment issues. But having strictly prescribed quid pro quo sex did produce significant sparks. It brought us back to the bargaining table. I think we have a lousy marriage, but at least we are having some decent sex while we figure out the rest of it."

From her husband, "I like her better when we fuck."

✳ *The Timer*

Meredith was drawn to his presence. Michel radiated a sense of self-confidence and power—and his French accent certainly didn't detract from his desirability. She was at a point in her life where she wanted a commitment from a suitable man. He wanted an American wife and a two-continent lifestyle. Meredith was beautiful, intelligent, accomplished. Later he would say derisively it was an international merger, not a marriage.

"We never have sex anymore," she said.

"The sex was never that good," he said.

They were in Paris when she told him, "If you don't fuck me, I'm out of here."

Without saying a word, he stormed out of the bedroom. She heard him slamming cabinets in the kitchen and wondered what he thought he was doing. Michel did not cook. And the liquor was in the library, the wine in a temperature-controlled storage vault off the hallway.

He walked back into their bedroom holding an egg timer aloft. *That stupid timer,* she thought, a gift from his *grand-mère,* hand-blown glass filled with sand that took exactly three minutes to flow from one end to the other.

"How long do you want me to fuck you?" he asked.

"See how far you get in three minutes," she retorted.

He put the timer down on the night table and grabbed her roughly in his arms.

She kept her eye on the timer as he kissed her, little nibbling bites and sucks from her neck down to the tops of her breasts. He took one nipple in his mouth, encircled it with his teeth, and pinched the other nipple between two fingers. Her heart was pounding in her ears as she fumbled with buttons, hers and his.

The sand had run through. She pulled back. So did he.

"Do you wish me to continue?" he asked.

For answer, she turned the timer over and pushed him down on the bed. Straddling him, she gave his nipples the same treatment he'd given hers. With his eye on the timer, he moaned in appreciation. When the three minutes were up, they were both naked from the waist up, little rivulets of comingled sweat trickling down their bodies.

He flipped the timer and his wife.

She grasped his erection through his pants. He was huge. She wanted him. He moved on top of her, simulating intercourse until she ached from wanting him inside her.

"Fuck me now," she said.

"Please," he insisted.

"Please," she whimpered.

She rolled on top of him, flipping the timer over in one smooth motion as she did. Struggling out of their pants, they kissed hungrily, greedily, sucking in the flesh of each other's lips and tongues, breasts and genitals with hot, angry mouths. Holding her hips, he guided her down on top of him. She screamed in delight.

Her spasms began seconds later.

Neither of them noticed the timer after that.

* *Part VIII* ....

FANTASY

eighteen ···

"I Shared My Fantasies— and She/He Isn't Speaking to Me Anymore."

Fantasies are out there in the open now. People talk about them. Men and women own up to having fantasies. A mere generation ago everyone was more circumspect about private sex thoughts and dreams. Men and especially women feared sounding like a deviant or turning off their partners if they confessed to, for example, fantasizing a group sex or S/M encounter.

If once lovers erred on the side of caution where fantasies are concerned, now they may be talking too much. And why not? Living as we do in a post-Oprah world, we all talk too much about every aspect of our private/sexual lives these days. Whatever happened to the concept of projecting an aura of mystery?

When sex experts (me included) tell you to share fantasies, we really mean: Make up fantasies and share them

·····

with your partner. Invent erotic stories and tell them to each other. We don't mean: Share with her that fantasy you have about her sister, or share with him that fantasy you have about his best friend, or spill the one about your ex-lover that you use every time you feel your arousal flagging during sex. Did you think we were telling you to do that?

Big mistake. Too much information!

The Standard Advice

Therapists suggest therapy and sexperts advise quid pro quo: Your partner gets to share a fantasy you won't like to hear to get even with you for hurting his or her feelings.

The revenge sharing is pointless. It won't get you where you want to be: in bed, having better-than-ordinary sex. You were hoping to jump-start your sex life when you shared that fantasy, weren't you? Get back to the goal.

There is, however, another reason that one shares a fantasy the partner clearly doesn't want to hear. You were trying to shake things up by making him or her jealous—or you were letting your partner know that you are very interested in another person. That's the fantasy-as-relationship-weapon scenario.

Sometimes the fantasy shared (and usually by women) is the one about the emotional lover. You probably work with him, and you definitely have a crush on him. Like a giddy teenager in love, you have to throw out hints because you secretly want everyone to know you're in crush mode. You just can't stop saying his name in conversation—with any-one. In that state of derangement, you "shared" with your husband. I would never suggest doing that, but it's too late now. Maybe getting this nonsense out in the open will have an upside: You'll see that a crush is just a crush before you do lasting harm to the marriage (or serious relationship).

But don't squelch your fantasies altogether. An active fantasy life—private, shared, acted out, or preferably a com-bination thereof—is one of the keys to keeping sex fun and interesting. That is particularly true if you are in a long-term monogamous relationship. Flirting with that emo-tional lover, even having a small crush on him, can be good for the relationship—if you don't take the crush/fantasy se-riously and use it to feed your desire for and arousal with your partner.

The Instant First-night Makeover: Apologize/Lie/Suck Up

If you haven't apologized profusely, do so now.

Apology not accepted? Lie if you must lie to move beyond the how-could-you/why-did-you phase. Say, "I made up that fantasy to make you jealous, get even with you for _____(fill in the blank), or because I read that men/women really got off on hearing that their partner fan-tasizes screwing their parents/sibling/best friend."

Indeed, some people do get off on hearing that their partners fantasize about having sex with another person. You're on safe psychological ground here.

Apology still not accepted? Suck up. You've never loved anyone the way you love him/her who is more handsome/beautiful than the object of your flimsy fantasy.

Now suck. See the directions for cunnilingus on page 113 and fellatio on page 121. Additional showy moves are on pages 113–114 and 124–125.

Give her multiple orgasms.

And for him, swallow. (See page 60.)

The Sex Life Makeover Plan

1. Go back and do it right.

Sharing fantasies is an exciting erotic game. Don't abandon the idea. Get it right this time.

❋Technique Tips

Never *admit to fantasizing about your partner's siblings, parent, best friends. If you've already done that, your story is: "I was just trying to get a reaction out of you." Don't back down from that story even under torture.*

Don't admit that you fantasize about someone else while the two of you make love—unless you know that your partner is aroused by fantasies of you with someone else. Otherwise, that's the you're-really-in-big-trouble-now fantasy. In truth, everyone fantasizes about another partner occasionally. If you do it more than occasionally and always with the same other person, you're probably

*using the fantasy lover as a wedge between you and your
partner. That's not healthy. Start gradually phasing that
person out of your erotic head now.*

*As I was saying, everyone does it occasionally, but
only fools acknowledge that.*

Never *share a fantasy about a man with a big penis if
his is small or a woman with luscious breasts if hers are
not. Instead, weave your partner's best physical traits
into the shared fantasy.*

*Fantasizing together during sex can be very hot. But
make your partner the object of that fantasy and talk it
out.*

*If you've pushed your partner to share a fantasy, don't
ridicule that fantasy. Imagine you are the one who ad-
mits after years of secret fantasizing that you want to
have sex on the steps of the Lincoln Memorial—only to
have your significant other shriek, "What, are you crazy?
That's sick!"*

2. Ask for a new sex move—an embellishment of a move
she/he does well—and incorporate that into a fantasy to
share.

Don't tell her you're dreaming about ultimate fellatio if
her basic blow job barely passes scrutiny. Set that issue of
oral gratification aside for the moment. Equate your fantasy
with perfecting her (or his) best skill.

3. Fantasy-of-the-month club

Agree to make up a new fantasy for sharing every month. Choose, for example, the first Saturday night of every month for fantasy sharing. Like that children's game of "I'll show you mine if you show me yours," you trade stories. Initially, this may seem awkward. But you will find that just talking about hot sex scenarios improves your sex life.

4. Use your fantasies to fuel your desire for your partner by making him or her your fantasy lover.

There are ways to bring your partner into the fantasy in your head. Find traits in him, for example, that are similar to those of your fantasy lover—the guy in the office across the hall. Do they both have strong jawlines? Broad shoulders? Focus on the similarities. At the point of highest arousal, replace the lover's face with your partner's.

What Sex Life Makeover Participants Say

"I used emotional lovers to keep a distance between me and my husband—and I did it for years. That was stupid. Once I learned how to fantasize the emotional lover to get aroused for sex with my husband, everything changed. I got closer to him. We are having better sex. And I don't fantasize about the men when I should be working or enjoying a good book."

And from a man: "I made the mistake of sharing my fantasies about being dominated with a longtime girlfriend. She thought I was sick and weird and it changed things between us. Now I keep the hard stuff to myself. When my wife   265

Fantasy

says, 'Tell me what you're fantasizing,' I say, 'Sex on the
beach at sunset with you, honey.' "

✳ Loving Brad

When Lynne met Brad she understood love at first sight. He was
beautiful. *I never described a man as beautiful before in my life,* she
wrote in her journal. *Brad is beautiful.* Thick dark hair, big brown
eyes, olive skin, tall, well built—he was perfect. She lived for the
days when she could see the dark mat of his chest hair through his
white shirt. *He must run out of clean undershirts every eight or nine
days,* she wrote, *and it just drives me up the wall, knowing only a few
buttons stand between me and his chest hair.*

She made excuses to walk by his cubicle just so she could say,
"Hey, Brad," and exchange some comments about the weather,
the home team, or something about work.

"Don't make a fool of yourself over that boy, Lynne," Carol, her
best friend at work, admonished her.

"He's not a boy," she said, not even caring that her crush was
that obvious.

He was maybe ten, fifteen years younger than Lynne, not a boy.
In meetings, she fantasized being alone in the office with him. He
would rip off her little black silk G-string and take her against the
wall, fuck her crazy, with her leg wrapped around his waist, her
hands on his high, tight butt. Working at her desk, with her panties
wet from wanting him, she imagined taking him in her mouth, his

penis eight, nine inches long and thick, harder than anything she'd ever experienced. Yes, she would let him fuck her in the ass, and she would love every painful moment of it.

"What's wrong with you lately?" her husband, Tom, asked. She was sitting across the kitchen table from him, but she wasn't really there. "You always look like you're somewhere else."

"Lot goin' on at work," she said, shoving mashed potatoes into her mouth as if she wanted them.

"You have to leave work at work," he said.

After dinner, he insisted on cleaning up the kitchen so she could relax. She went into the TV room, pulled her journal from beneath a cushion, and wrote about Brad. *He looked at me with such smoldering eyes that my nipples got hard.* Suddenly she looked up and saw Tom.

"In the mood?" he asked.

"Headache," she said.

Several days went by. She avoided sex with Tom as much as possible because it didn't feel right with him anymore. His hands on her body were rough, awkward. Brad, in her dreams, touched her the way she wanted to be touched. He parted her labia lips with his tongue and brought her to orgasm with the bridge of his nose against her clit.

"You should see a doctor," Tom said, interrupting the thoughts she was putting down in her journal.

Brad had her nipple in his mouth and his hand was caressing her inner thigh.

"A doctor?" she said.

"You've lost interest in sex, Lynne. Something's wrong."

"Lot goin' on at work," she mumbled.

Brad's fingers had found her G-spot. She squirmed on the sofa.

More days passed. She contrived to be in the elevator with Brad. They got on at the twentieth floor with two other people. By the seventh floor, they were alone. Heart racing, senses tingling, she knew that he felt her presence as keenly as she did his. She could smell a note of sandalwood in his cologne.

"Lynne," he said. "There's something I want to tell you."

"Yes," she whispered, turning to face him, the love shining in her eyes. "You can tell me anything."

"I'm gay," he said. She laughed. He was kidding, wasn't he? His face reddened—in embarrassment? Anger? "I'm gay," he repeated. "Look, I wouldn't be comfortable with you mooning over me if I were straight. But the fact is, I'm gay. And you're married." The door opened on the ground floor. "Your husband sounds like a great guy," he said, brushing past her.

She ran to the parking lot, got into her car, and drove straight home. Furiously she pulled her journal out from the sofa cushion and threw it into the trash. She cried and cursed herself for being such a fool. When Tom came home, she told him she'd messed up a project at work. He held her in his arms and stroked her hair and back while she cried some more.

That night she dreamed about Brad. She was at her favorite part, where he unzipped his pants, exposing what she had described in her journal as his throbbing manhood. Breathing hard, she rolled over closer to Tom and rubbed her hot groin against him. Soon his manhood was throbbing.

"Make love to me, baby," she said.

When he entered her, she was overcome with desire for him. *Yes,* she thought, *fuck my brains out.* Afterward, she was grateful to be back.

She ignored Brad at work unless she had to talk to him. But she kept him around in her fantasy life. Sometimes it was the three of them in bed: her, Tom, and Brad. In her version of the story, however, Brad was definitely not gay.

"She/He Wants to Act Out
Fantasies, and I Don't."

Acting out fantasies is a favorite sexual game of the respondents to *Men's Health* magazine sex surveys. And they are not alone. Sophisticated lovers eventually get around to sexual theater. But if you read the previous chapter, you realize that acting out fantasies doesn't necessarily mean acting out *your* fantasies—or at least not the private ones you use to arouse yourself.

The Standard Advice

Therapists typically say: Don't try to act out those fantasies. Sexperts say: Proceed with caution.

Reasonable advice all around. There are some good reasons for not acting out fantasies. First, they can lose the power to arouse if you bring them out of your mental closet.

Second, the logistics or mechanics might not work at all in real life. And third, it is often the *idea* of bondage, pain, group sex, or whatever that thrills us, not the reality.

More important, your private fantasies can really turn off your partner.

Nancy Friday, the doyenne of fantasies, once said, "For every person who has written to me about the joys of performing their sex dreams in reality, there have been three or four who knew in advance that it wouldn't work, or who tried it and were disappointed."

Yet all this good advice leaves you hanging on the tenterhooks of your own desire if you are craving fantasy action. Should you retreat into the private fantasy garden and never try to bring your partner in there with you? No. You can act out fantasies—but likely not the ones you use during masturbation or to become aroused again when you've lost it during sex with your partner. Bring some beautiful new tropical plants into that garden before inviting company over.

The Instant First-night Makeover: Let Her/Him Write the Script

The reluctant partner agrees to act out a fantasy—but she/he writes the script and directs the action. Develop a fantasy scenario that has the elements most important to your partner, but still acceptable to you. Otherwise you'll feel silly, not sexy. Make the story a hot one. Even the most reluctant fantasy player usually gets aroused if the script is right.

Break the questionable fantasy down into content elements. If your partner, for example, fantasizes a bondage scenario and you object to that, ask yourself why. Are you upset because his (or her) sexual imagery isn't politically correct? Talk through those issues and try to get them out of your sex life. It helps to understand that bondage, again for example, represents freedom from responsibility.

Use costumes and props. A Sex Life Makeover couple who agreed to act out a Gilligan's Island fantasy—she was Ginger; he was the professor—dressed their parts. It's hard to pretend you're a glamorous movie star if you don't even put on lipstick and heels.

Look for ways to compromise and camouflage. You fantasize being dominated. Call it "swept off your feet," conjuring that famous image of Rhett carrying Scarlett up the staircase. Have him toss you onto the bed.

Work from a real script. Some people have trouble getting in touch with their inner erotic creativity. Act out a story you've read or a scene from a video or DVD.

The Sex Life Makeover Plan

1. Expand your mental erotic horizons.

Read and watch erotica. And don't stop there. Some mainstream and literary novels and films have great sexy bits. When you come across an erotic passage in a novel, put a bookmark at the page and read it aloud to your lover later.

2. Take turns playing each other's favorite film (or fiction) character.

Princess Leia from the first *Star Wars* series is a great favorite with thirty-something men. Do your hair in those twin buns and buy a gold lamé bikini. (If you do that for him, he has to play Han Solo opposite you.)

3. Play gigolo/whore.

Pretend that one partner is buying the services of the other. Dress your parts. Meet as "strangers" at a bar and negotiate the deal. What are the fees? Exactly what do you get for the money? Stick to the terms. And stay in character throughout the sexual encounter.

4. Talk out your fantasies through phone sex.

If neither one of you travels on business, have phone sex with each of you in separate rooms of the house. Some people find phone sex liberating because they are not inhibited by the presence of the other.

✳ **Technique Tips** ....

Start with something easy like, "What are you wearing?" Make the answer to that and every question as detailed and sensual as possible. Say, for example, "I'm wearing a black silk shirt unbuttoned to the navel. The fabric clings to my breasts. I'm not wearing underwear."

Don't use words that you can't say comfortably. If

cock *and* pussy *don't roll off your tongue, use* penis *and* vagina.

Talk about sex acts that you know turn your partner on.

Get specific. The more details, the better. Where do you want him to put it? How hard? What's he doing with his mouth? His hands?

Bring in a surprise scenario. Play to his hidden fantasies. Maybe he's never asked if he can ejaculate on your body, but you've seen how hungrily he watches those scenes in porn films.

Masturbate. Faked moans and groans are nice. But why not experience the real thing?

What Sex Life Makeover Participants Say

"Acting out fantasies is a great way to shake things up sexually. When you act out a part, you let go of attitudes or inhibitions that were keeping you back. Being a typical man, I thought I'd feel silly pretending to be a pirate ravishing my wife, but I really got into it."

And she says: "I love sexual theater. I am a frustrated creative person in a dull job that pays well. This is my outlet. I love it."

✳ The Chauffeur

Nervously biting her lip, Lauren scanned the group of waiting drivers in the baggage claim area at O'Hare airport. Where was he? All of those men holding signs and none with her name on it! She was about ready to pull out her cell phone when she spotted him. Cap at an angle on his head, he signaled to her from the edge of the crowd.

"Driver, you're late," she snapped, putting the handle to her roller bag in his hand.

"Follow me, ma'am," he said, pulling the bag ahead of her. A blast of Chicago winter whistled up her skirt and slapped her bare waxed pussy. Home. "Did you have good weather in Los Angeles?" he asked.

Admiring his butt as he walked ahead of her, she bit back the acid comment she almost made in response. He was tall, dark, and handsome, with the build and stride of an athlete. And she was horny. She moved close to him as he opened her door and let her fur coat fall open and one soft silk-covered breast graze his hand. He helped her into the backseat, stowed her bag in the trunk, and got behind the wheel. She picked up the phone and asked him to open the partition between them.

"Yes, ma'am?" he said.

"Driver, your boss called to say he's running late for our meeting." She met his eyes in the mirror and read amusement in them. "I have an hour to kill. I'd like you to entertain me."

"And how do you like to be entertained, ma'am?"

"That depends. How big is your cock?"

"My cock, ma'am, is almost ten inches long."

"I see." She hiked her skirt and spread her legs so that he could see. "Drive to the IHOP a mile from here." She moistened her fingers with her own saliva and touched herself. "Do you know it?"

Without replying, he pulled the car out of its space. She masturbated slowly as he drove, occasionally pulling her fingers away so he could see her glistening lips in the mirror. He parked the car at the back of the IHOP lot and joined her in the backseat.

"You have an impressive hard-on," she whispered, slightly out of breath.

"You have an impressive pussy, ma'am," he said. "May I touch it?"

"Suck it," she said, taking his head in her hands and roughly pushing him down into her genitals.

Eagerly he began eating her out with long, slow strokes of his tongue inside her lips. He made circles around her clitoris with the tip of his tongue until she lost sense of whether he was licking in a clockwise or counterclockwise direction. Then he covered her clitoris with his mouth and gently sucked while his fingers plied her G-spot.

The orgasms started in both places and met in the middle, crashing like ocean waves, knocking her back. She was so excited that she didn't realize she'd been holding his ears until he carefully pried her fingers loose. But he stayed down there, pulling orgasm after orgasm out of her with his fingers and tongue.

When he came up, his face was glazed with her. Groaning, he unzipped his pants, exposing a penis that, if not quite ten inches long, was beautifully erect.

"Fuck me," she demanded breathlessly.

He plunged into her forcefully. A few strokes later, she was gone again. She felt the thundering surge of his climax and the blood pounding in her ears at the same time, as if everything inside her had turned to molten liquid. This was the best sex she'd ever had.

They lay entwined, catching their breath, freezing their asses off.

"We should take this car back to the rental place," he said. "Get a cab home and build a fire."

"Yes," she agreed. Nuzzling his hairline affectionately, she told him how much she'd missed him. "Honey," she said as he zipped up, "did you remember to take the cat to the vet for her shot?"

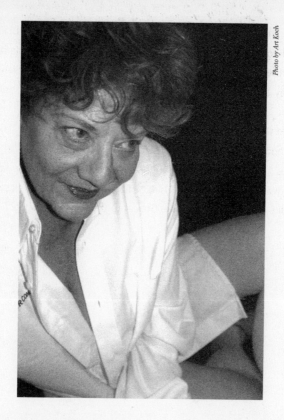

Photo by Art Koch

SUSAN CRAIN BAKOS, a licensed sex educator, is an internationally recognized sex authority and author of eight books, including *Sexational Secrets: The Ultimate Guide for Erotic Know-How*. Her articles have appeared in every major American women's magazine, and for seven years, she was a contributing editor and columnist at *Penthouse Forum*. She has appeared on *Oprah, Good Morning America, Jenny Jones*, and numerous other television and radio shows.